1. Great black-backed gull
2. Black-headed gull
3. Chaffinch
4. Small tortoiseshell
5. Pearl-bordered fritillary
6. Red admiral

7. Hemlock water dropwort
8. Common mallow
9. Sea aster
10. Broad buckler fern
11. Foxglove

Somerset and North Devon Coast Path

Clive Gunnell

Long-Distance Footpath Guide No 10

London: Her Majesty's Stationery Office

Published for the Countryside Commission

Pages vi–vii Bossington Hill

The maps in this guide are extracts from Ordnance Survey 1:50,000 maps (about 1¼ in. to the mile) and have been prepared from O.S. sheets 180, 181, 190.

Drawings: Louis Mackay

Photographs: Chris Chapman

Long-distance footpath guides published for the Countryside Commission by HMSO:

The Pennine Way, by Tom Stephenson: 120 pages, £3·95 net

The Cleveland Way, by Alan Falconer: 144 pages, £2·95 net

The Pembrokeshire Coast Path, by John H Barrett: 124 pages, £2·95 net

Offa's Dyke Path, by John B Jones: 124 pages, £2·95 net

The Ridgeway Path, by Seán Jennett: 120 pages, £2·95 net

Cornwall Coast Path, by Edward C Pyatt: 120 pages, £3·95 net

South Downs Way, by Seán Jennett: 122 pages, £2·95 net

Dorset Coast Path, by Brian Jackman: 122 pages, £2·95 net

South Devon Coast Path, by Brian Le Messurier: 122 pages, £2·95 net

In preparation:
North Downs Way
Wolds Way

Government Bookshops:
49 High Holborn, London W1CV 6HB
13a Castle Street, Edinburgh EH2 3AR
41 The Hayes, Cardiff CF1 1JW
Brazennose Street, Manchester M60 8AS
Southey House, Wine Street, Bristol BS1 2BQ
258 Broad Street, Birmingham B1 2HE
80 Chichester Street, Belfast BT1 4JY

Government publications are also available through booksellers

Prepared for the Countryside Commission by the Central Office of Information.

Countryside Commission, John Dower House, Crescent Place, Cheltenham, Glos. GL50 3RA

The waymark sign is used in plaque or stencil form by the Countryside Commission on long-distance footpaths

Printed in England for Her Majesty's Stationery Office by Burgess & Son (Abingdon) Ltd. Abingdon Oxon
ISBN 0 11 700904 0   Dd   696383   C250

Contents

Introduction

My introduction to the Somerset and North Devon Coast Path occurred through my work as a documentary film maker. Some years ago I was asked by Westward Television to make a series of films covering the whole of the South West Peninsula Coast Path, beginning at Minehead in Somerset and ending at South Haven Point, close to the entrance of Poole harbour in Dorset.

The experience of making these films instilled in me a great love for the Somerset and North Devon coast and helped me to fully appreciate its splendours.

There are short passages along this section of Coast Path where no official route exists, notably between Braunton and Westward Ho! Here I have tried to suggest alternative walks which would I believe prove interesting, and would open up facets of the North Devon countryside and coastline which might otherwise remain unknown to the walker.

This Path contains some of the most beautiful and varied coastal scenery to be found anywhere in the world. The route is well charted with acorn symbolled signposts, blazed trees and, on occasion, slates or granite stones set into the ground. On the more difficult climbs and descents, wooden steps have been fashioned by the Wardens. Across the Exmoor National Park section, which stretches from Minehead to Combe Martin, the custodians have done a splendid job of route marking, and I do not believe it possible for anyone to take a wrong turning.

The 824 kilometres of the South West Peninsula Coast Path make it the longest footpath in Britain. The Somerset and North Devon section covers 132 kilometres, although this will vary depending on the number of alternative

routes undertaken, and does not include the stretch between Braunton and Westward Ho!

The idea for the Coast Path originated from a report published in 1945, written by John Dower and entitled *National Parks of England and Wales*. In 1947 the already existing National Parks Committee suggested there should be a continuous path – following the cliff edge wherever possible – along the route of the old coastguard tracks, and the detailed work of creating such a path began in 1949 with the setting up of the National Parks Commission. The Somerset and North Devon Coast Path route was approved by the Secretary of State for the Environment on 13 January 1961 and officially opened on 20 May 1978 by Denis Howell, then Minister of State in the Department of the Environment. He spoke of Hugh Dalton who campaigned hard and long for public access to our coastal landscape. Lord Winstanley, Chairman of the Countryside Commission, paid tribute in his speech to the work of Arthur Blenkinsop M.P., who devoted years of his parliamentary life to the same end.

When I set out once again to walk the route from Minehead to Marsland Mouth it was with the firm intention of doing it in easy stages, never covering more than 20 kilometres in one day – often less. There is so much to appreciate, enjoy and understand.

My thanks are due to my wife, Elizabeth, who conveyed me backwards and forwards each morning and evening, and then surprised me by arriving at remote and assumed inaccessible points along the route bearing gifts of hot pasties and cold beer, thus providing a sumptuous lunch-break for us both.

CG

Hints and advice

Walking has become an essential part of the outdoor leisure activities of a growing band of enthusiasts for whom it provides a release from the ever-increasing pressures of over-crowding, high-rise living and perpetual conflict that have become an inescapable element of life in all large conurbations. Out in the open the walker can relax and re-charge batteries.

Another reason for the growing popularity of walking is because it is, perhaps erroneously, believed that very little is required by way of specialized knowledge or equipment. Although I have stated that the Path is not difficult to follow, there are places where the ability to map-read and take a compass bearing would help the walker enormously, and relieve a certain amount of anxiety.

Ordnance Survey maps at a scale no less than 1:50,000 (approximately 1¼ inches to the mile) will be helpful in addition to the maps contained in this book to give a wider view of the country around the Path.

Exmoor National Park also publish a guide book to their section of the Path which is available from Park Information Centres at Minehead, Lynmouth and Combe Martin.

Clothing is an important item to which the walker should pay great attention. It is essential to carry, if not always necessary to wear, clothes that offer protection from the elements and, at the same time, keep the body at an efficient temperature. Many walkers fail to realise that exposure does not require arctic conditions, but often occurs in comparatively mild temperatures if the body is not adequately protected against the wind and rain. In the same manner, walking stripped to the waist on a hot summer day can very quickly bring on intense headaches and nausea as well as painful sunburn. The sun's rays, filtered through the brine-soaked atmosphere, will eventually cause heat exhaustion. Always wear a shirt and a light-weight hat of some kind however warm the day, and at all other times follow these rules.

Wear a vest and woollen shirt over which you can pull a

Rocky coastline near Hartland

1

woollen sweater – it is simple to take them off and put them in your rucksack – and always carry an extra woollen sweater for emergencies. Trousers should also be of a material strong enough to provide protection against brambles, stinging nettles and the occasional blackthorn, and also to keep out the wind. Denim is not suitable, and when wet becomes impossible to walk in. Most outdoor equipment shops sell woollen trousers especially for walking or climbing. However, if you do not want to incur this expense stout corduroy or whipcord trousers will do. I also carry nylon over-trousers which can easily be put on in a rain storm or where the path, as it often does, goes through knee-high bracken soaked by a recent shower. An anorak is essential; light-weight is preferable, but it must keep out the wind and the rain and come down to the top of the thighs.

Finally the feet: remember the adage of all old infantry-men 'look after your feet and they will look after you'. Wear woollen socks always, never nylon. Two pairs are better than one and are very comfortable. Boots are without doubt the most important item of all. Good, strong walking boots that protect the feet from rough, uneven ground and sharp flints, having commando or similar pattern soles with a deep tread providing a safe grip on all surfaces and, of course, protecting the ankles against twisting or turning over. These can be an ex-pensive item but well worth it for they will last a long time.

The last requirement is a rucksack. It should be large enough to carry a spare woollen jersey and such clothing as may be removed along the way in warm weather, or be needed in very wet weather. Also it should contain maps, a compass, first aid kit (I needed two elastic bandages on this journey), a torch which can be used for map-reading at night or to signal in an emergency, and a whistle. The international mountain distress signal is six blasts on the whistle repeated at minute intervals. The food and refreshment carried is obviously a personal choice. I like to have a flask of hot tea, fruit – dried and fresh – and chocolate.

But the most important requirement on any walk is common sense. It is common sense that prevents a walker from attempting dangerous rock climbs or scrambles; from going too close to what could be a crumbling cliff edge or unsafe overhang, or from deliberately tempting fate by trying to experience the pleasure of a high cliff-top view despite a fear of heights. Don't do these things, or go bathing – however tempting the water may look – without first enquiring about tides, currents and dangerous undertows. Be sure if you attempt a beach traverse that the tide is on the ebb, and always remember these points:

Know exactly where you are on the map at all times.

Make sure someone is always aware of the route you have taken and your expected time of arrival.

Wind is your enemy – coupled with rain it can threaten survival. So look for shelter behind rocks, banks or hedgerows and put on all the warm clothing you possess.

You can detect exposure in your companions by these signs: complaints of tiredness, cold, excessive shivering, loss of colour, a marked mental deterioration combined with an inability to walk properly and any unreasonable behaviour. Keep the sufferer warm by wrapping him in extra clothing and giving hot drinks. Never give alcohol, rub the limbs nor apply local heat, and do not allow the sufferer to continue walking even though he insists he feels better.

Rocks, animals, men and ships

Rocks

Three hundred and fifty million years ago the whole region covering the Somerset and North Devon Coast Path was under water. Beneath this sea great thicknesses of sediment slowly accumulated – marine slimes with sand, limestone, shale and hard grits. These sediments spread rapidly in shallow water from the south-west, helped by sporadic outbursts of volcanic action during the Lower Devonian period. In North Devon and Somerset the oldest Devonian rocks are the Lynton Beds which consist of fine-grained laminated mud and sandstone 400 metres thick, with a slender shell bed.

In the area between Barnstaple and Minehead the Devonian succession exhibits an alternate pattern of marine and Continental geological conditions, beginning with Lower Devonian and continuing through Middle and Upper Devonian – all bearing quantities of marine fossils. Unfortunately earth movements of later periods seriously damaged the rock formations and fossils and, as a consequence, this area does not lend its name to a major division of geological time.

This was a period of shallow seas and dry land, when the landscape took on a shape and pattern totally different from any that had been there before. An enormous land-mass developed with high mountain chains stretching from southern Ireland to Norway, whilst the sediment that had previously grown under the sea began to build up on dry land, providing us for the first time with a record of land organisms. The emergence of such great areas of dry land in the Devonian period resulted in important biological changes, bringing about the evolution of land plants which, in their turn, provided the vegetation necessary for the existence of land animals. The delicately tissued remains of one of the oldest known land plants was discovered in rock strata of the Middle Devonian age. It was perfectly preserved in peat, petrified into a rock of almost pure silica – known as chert. Discovered before the first world war by geologist Dr. Mackie, it was named Rhynie Chert after an area of Devonian volcanic rock

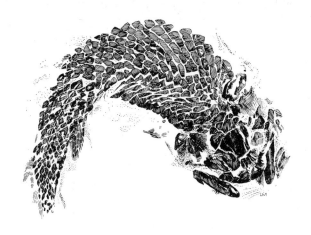

Fossil fish from the Devonian Old Red Sandstone

near Rhynie in Aberdeenshire. It was an undoubted land plant containing central strands of woody tissue to hold it erect, pores for passing gasses in and out, and it had a device for scattering spores into the air to be dispersed by the wind.

By the end of the Devonian period two new groups of fish had also made their appearance. Earlier fish had been predominantly slow, bulky, bottom feeding creatures finding food in the mud and sediment of the ocean floor, shovelling it up with scoop-like mouths. These fish carried their bone structure externally. The new cartilaginous fish, such as sharks, had no bone skeleton; those that had, developed it internally and their shovel-like mouths evolved into jaws, thus creating the fish still dominant in our oceans today.

The Devonian was followed by the Carboniferous period when the area was subjected to enormous movements of earth – cracking, twisting and fracturing the rock created from the sediment into anticlines and overturned folds, interspersed with faults and fractures that are visible today running in an east-south-east direction, imprinting a characteristic 'grain' to the area from Hartland Point along the coast to Cornwall. This uplifting of the earth was followed by a period of intense erosion with dry, arid conditions, resulting in the deposit of Triassic sediments – the New Red Sandstone of the Vale of Porlock that rests uncomfortably on the Devonian rock to form a low fertile valley of coarse rockstone, sandstone and marls or mudstones, predominantly red in colour.

The succeeding Jurassic formations consisted of marine deposits of lias clay and limestone alternating with shales containing ammonites indicating another inundation by the sea over this area, after the Continental period

5

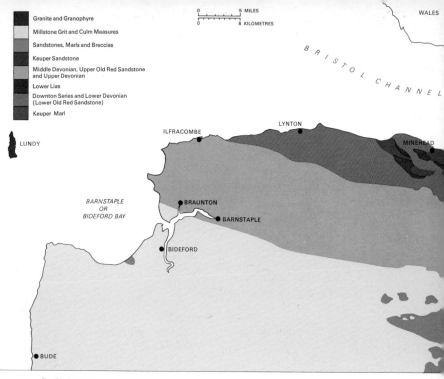

Geological map

represented by the rocks of New Red Sandstone. They form the furthest westerly situation of this Jurassic strata and are preserved at Selworthy and repeated in exposed cliffs near Watchet.

At a much later period drifts and superficial deposits occurred. During the Great Ice Age the coastal area from Somerset to Cornwall was put under intense pressure by ice sheets which, in places, encroached some distance inland. The land froze for long periods, and then the coming of the thaw brought down from the high ground large masses of fragmentary rocks and boulders to form 'head' deposits. A mixture of clay and frost-shattered stones, which sludged down even gentle inclines, caused a rounding off and lowering of the slopes in this area.

Mineral deposits in the region consisting of iron lodes, manganese and copper ore were confined to a belt traversing Exmoor following the west-north-west trend of Devonian strata from the Brendon Hills to an area around Simonsbath. Iron and copper ore was also worked at North Molton, but Exmoor has, in its time, yielded up small quantities of manganese, antimony, lead, zinc and even gold. That time finally ceased at the end of the nineteenth century as the workings became uneconomical. During the thirteenth century silver and lead deposits were first discovered at Combe Martin and, upon the marriage of Eleanor, daughter of Edward I, to the Count de Barre, a dowry of 270 lbs. of silver was supplied from Combe Martin. In Elizabethan times a new rich lode was uncovered, and it is said that Queen Victoria owned and wore several brooches made from Combe Martin silver.

The area today consists of smoothly moulded hills with little or no bare rock displayed, other than along the route of the Coast Path and a few isolated Exmoor heights. Eastward the Brendons constitute a high plateau of cultivated countryside, large agricultural fields separated by earth and stone walls topped with beech hedges; scattered stone farm dwellings and forests of conifer. Inland the 520 metres of Dunkery Beacon impose their massive presence indicating the formation of a series of bold uplands running north west across the National Park. This cloud-catching dome is the main water source, producing an annual rainfall of up to 150 centimetres a year, creating numerous rivers and streams swiftly dropping and plunging northwards through water slides and pools to provide the spectacular waterfalls of the coast walk. Away to the south, leaving the watershed, the rivers Exe and Barle take a more leisurely and gentle course, meandering their way across the breadth of Devon, providing excellent facilities for salmon and trout fishing, before reaching the coast at Exmouth and Exeter.

Animals

All streams crossed on the journey from Minehead to Cornwall contain trout which can often be observed upstream flashing in the clear waters of inland pools, whilst salmon lurk in their lower reaches. Hotels and inns along the way cater for the needs of all anglers.

These same streams provide an ideal situation for families of otters still surviving in Somerset and North Devon, particularly on Exmoor, which provides sanctuary for a magnificent variety of wildlife unequalled elsewhere in the South West. The last great herds of wild deer left in England, between 600 and 1,000 in number, roam the woods, blue moor grass and farmland. No more noble sight exists in the English October countryside than that of a mature stag with a fine 'head' after it has shed its 'velvet' (the tissue of blood-vessels covering and feeding the horn). The red deer is indigenous to this area, but other species have also made their homes in the safety of Exmoor National Park. Fallow deer can sometimes be seen in Woodcombe Brake at Minehead and around Dunster. Roe deer, which like the red deer are part of our ancient fauna, have been reported in Selworthy Woods and at Porlock where they live off shrubs and the tops of young trees, to the frustration of the foresters. Japanese sika deer, descendants of a number which escaped from

Red deer

Brown hare

Fox

Western gorse

Ling

Bell heather

Adder

Pixton Dulverton, now inhabit the southern borders of Exmoor in the woods lining the valley of the Mole and Bray. Roughly the same size as fallow deer, they can be distinguished in the summer by a pattern of white spots running along the reddish brown of their backs, and by a long white tail often with a slim black line along the centre.

Another native of this landscape is the small, hardy, Exmoor pony. The present breed are descended from the ponies rounded up in 1818 and sent to Ashway Farm, owned by Sir Thomas Dyke Acland, and run out on Winsford Hill to breed. Standing not much more than 12 hands, with a reddish brown coat running to dark brown, and with lighter coloured flanks, the pure bred Exmoor must have a biscuit coloured muzzle. Today, however, the Exmoor is facing a possibility of extinction owing to inbreeding.

The country has many foxes finding a good living off the numbers of brown hares and, despite myxomatosis, rabbits that flourish here. Badger sets and molehills testify to the continued existence of these animals, whilst mink – now declared indigenous – are as great a pest here as they have become in South Devon. Adders are widespread over Exmoor, especially in areas covered by gorse and heather and can be determined by their dirty, olive-brown colour with a dark zig-zag line along the back, and a 'V' or 'X' mark behind the head. Grass snakes, a harmless, non-poisonous olive green snake with oblong dots and orange patches behind the head, are found in Porlock Marsh and, seeking drier patches of heather and grass also, are the common lizard and slow-worm.

Exmoor ponies

The last official survey recorded 69 species of butterfly in Britain; the observant walker could, with a degree of luck, see 35 of these between Minehead and Marsland Mouth. The most common varieties are the small tortoiseshell, marsh fritillary, peacock, red admiral and small heath. On the Path above Heddon's Mouth I watched a number of large and dingy skippers and green hairstreak. The common blue seemed to be everywhere. Of the rare butterflies, the painted lady, clouded yellow, pearl bordered fritillary and holly blue have all been recorded. Among the varieties of moth common to the area are the elephant hawk, emperor, cream spot tiger and fox moth.

But the keen bird-watcher will achieve most satisfaction from this area because of the enormous variety of habitat provided by rugged coastline, wooded valleys with tumbling streams, wild moorland and cultivated fields. Over 100 different species of bird nest here each year. Almost the same number of rare birds visit the area, whilst winter visitors and passage migrants bring the number of birds that may be observed throughout the year to 243.

Green and great-spotted woodpeckers, treecreepers, redstarts, pied and spotted flycatchers, chiffchaffs, willow and wood warblers and nuthatches inhabit the old oak woodlands of the lower valleys. In the streams, herons

Green
woodpecker

Grey heron

Willow warbler

Spotted
flycatcher

Pied
flycatcher

Sessile oak

stand aloof from busy grey wagtails and energetic dippers, whilst the kingfisher prefers the slower running water of the Exe or Barle. On the high moorland, red and black grouse live happily with meadow pipits and skylarks, and wheatears, ring ouzels, winchats and cuckoos arrive to swell their numbers every spring. Buzzards soar and circle overhead; kestrels hover over open ground or perch on isolated hawthorn or on telegraph poles. Leaving Heddon's Mouth and again at Hartland Point I rejoiced in the sight of a peregrine falcon successfully stooping on to a feral pigeon. A more patient observer might be rewarded by the rare spectacle of a Montagu's harrier, hobby or red kite – all of which have been sighted over Exmoor in past years.

Of the nocturnal birds of prey the tawny, brown and wood owl are by far the most common, and are often found in woodland or copse close to human habitation. The barn owl is once again flourishing after almost disappearing from the area during the 60s due, it is believed, to extensive use of pesticides. The little owl, first reported on Exmoor in 1917, still survives although numbers are declining; a regular visitor during the months of autumn and winter is the short-eared owl. A pair of long-eared owls were recorded nesting on Exmoor in 1968, and a solitary snowy owl from the sub-arctic has been sighted during recent winters on Molland Common where it presumably survives on rabbits, small birds and possibly voles.

Above all the Coast Path provides the only possible way of viewing the increasing population of sea-birds. Some of these nest on cliff ledges in full view of the walker, but it is wise to remember that all our birds are protected by the Protection of Birds Act and it is an offence to kill them or remove young or eggs.

The herring gull outnumbers all other varieties, scavenging the outdoor beach cafés and dive-bombing picnicking tourists for food scraps. The herring gull is easily recognised by its pearl-grey mantle, black-tipped wings and a yellow bill with a red spot. It is also the sea-bird that follows the furrowing farmer. There are numbers of great black-backed gulls and the lesser black-backed gull is a regular summer visitor, whilst black-headed and common gulls are with us in the winter. Kittiwakes can be seen and heard, for the clear 'kittiwak' call cannot be confused with any other sea-bird. Between March and August the young of a small colony of fulmars, nesting in the Valley of Rocks, can be observed emerging from large single white eggs, surrounded by earth and turf on the cliff ledges. Diving seawards to swim under water catching fish are the last descendants of the extinct great auk – razorbills, and with them, of course, guillemots. The all-black colouring with white chin and thigh patches easily identifies the cormorant from its smaller, slimmer, dark-coloured diving companion, the shag. The shag has a lovely greenish sheen to its plumage and, during spring, sports a forward-pointing crest. All these birds flourish in the rocky inaccessibility of their cliff-side colonies where only the most skilful – or totally foolhardy – climber could penetrate, and in this way are protected from the ravages of that most successful and ruthless predator of all, man.

Men
Early Neolithic man seems to have avoided the north coast of Cornwall, Devon and Somerset, preferring to settle at Maiden Castle, Hembury, Haldon, Hazard Hill and Carn Brea in the south and west.

The beginning of the second millenium witnessed the arrival of the Beaker folk from Spain; warriors and hunters, their name derives from characteristic pottery vessels of highly ornamented thin red ware – the beaker. Evidence of these settlements exists in the form of such beakers, and burial cists found at Culbone and Wick, near Stogursey, on this coast.

People from the eastern Mediterranean arrived with metals, the technology to work them and knowledge of how to prospect the area for more. Discovering and exporting tin in this manner inaugurated the Bronze Age. The increasing requirements of fuel for smelting led to the deforestation of the South West, opening up large areas of land for agriculture. The kistvaens, menhirs, pounds and hut settlements probably date from Bronze Age times along with barrows and earthworks. Setta Barrow, Chapman Barrows, Caw Castle and Mounsey, alongside the Barle, the Caratacus Stone on Winsford Hill and the 'clapper' bridge at Tarr Steps are all possibly of this period. During the Bronze Age, Celtic immigrants arrived and established the Iron Age culture. They also established a system of forts, and splendid examples survive at Countisbury Hill and Bury Castle, near Selworthy. But the Iron Age population of the region was small and poverty stricken, living in isolated, undefended communities, running with families and livestock to the forts for safety when danger threatened.

The Romans established a garrison community at Exeter and built roads providing access to a handful of forts farther west. Old Barrow and Martinhoe Beacon over-looking the Bristol Channel, were occupied between A.D.48 and A.D.75. Subsequently the Anglo-Saxons settled in Devon, but not in Cornwall where the Celts remained dominant. Viking invaders also settled along the coastal strips in small communities, but never penetrated far inland.

Up to the present day the people of Somerset and North Devon have made a living almost entirely off the land or the sea, with only isolated incidents of mining for copper, lead, iron and silver. And so it is that throughout its entire

Pottery made by the Beaker folk

length from Minehead to Marsland Mouth the Coast Path
runs across farmland of some kind; even the gorse and
heather-clad undulations of Exmoor's high cliff-tops are
used for grazing sheep. The farm fields are separated by a
network of drystone-walls clinging tenaciously to the
hillsides in defiance of the ravages of time, and the movements of the earth beneath. Only the Coast Path is defined
by a series of wooden posts and wire mesh fencing. The
solid stone-built farms and outbuildings have been
occupied, often for centuries, by generations of the same
Somerset and North Devon families, and only today can
the infiltration of new blood be discerned in either the
farming community or their livestock.

From Minehead to Combe Martin the predominant
animal is the Exmoor sheep – a horned, hardy species with
a moderately long staple of wool, once used extensively by
the cloth manufacturers of North and South Molton,
Cullompton, Thorverton and Tiverton. Occasionally the
Scottish black-faced sheep can be seen, but these generally
graze further inland. This sheep was imported to Exmoor
over 80 years ago and has been successfully crossed with
the native breed. Along with the sheep came Scottish
shepherds who also remained in this area, and can still
be identified through names such as 'Little' to the present
day.

Travelling westwards through Ilfracombe and Woolacombe the breeds of sheep become more varied with the
introduction of the Devon close wool – a bigger sheep than
the Exmoor horn, and also a number of cross-breeds such
as the border Leicester ram and the Suffolk which are both
crossed with native stock.

Again on Exmoor the cattle will be almost exclusively
pure Devon beef, a breed becoming less popular in its

13

native area than elsewhere in the country; and the black Galloway is also a familiar sight from the Coast Path. Further west there are dairy herds of friesians with the inevitable Hereford cross, and nowadays it is not possible to walk very far without seeing evidence of the once very popular introduction to this country from France of the charollais bull – a popularity that seems to be on the wane.

Finally, there may be fields of wheatstraw, silage or hay bordering the Path; whilst the fertile valley of Porlock is extensively sown with barley. On the fields of the Taw/ Torridge estuary, fields of maize can be seen from the roadside of the supplementary walk between Braunton and Westward Ho! (see pages 58 – 61).

Ships

There are no deep-water harbours on this coast, but a number of small busy ports, which once carried on an extensive overseas and local trade. Appledore, Bideford, Barnstaple, Minehead and Watchet all had periods of prosperity. Watchet still prospers as a trading harbour. Appledore is internationally famous for shipbuilding, both for its modern, totally covered shipyards, and for the traditional method of making wooden ships which is still carried on here. The seamen of Appledore were famous throughout the world. In 1700 over half the nation's wool imports from Ireland came into Appledore in its 40 locally-owned ships. Between 1786 and 1818, 77 vessels were built to carry immigrants to the New World and return with timber. By the turn of the century over 50 vessels would cross the bar together on one tide – which must have been a magnificent sight. Equally magnificent were the sailing barges of the Taw/Torridge estuary. Between 6 and 15 metres long, with large hatches and short fore and aft decks, they had masts cut down and stepped in tabernacles to facilitate lowering when passing under road bridges and the railway bridge at Fremington. Rigged with a gaff mainsail and staysail they sailed out to the gravel banks off Crow Point and anchored, waiting for the ebbing tide to leave them stranded and aground. The crews began the back-breaking task of loading the barge full of wet sand and gravel, sometimes barely completed before the rising tide rocked the barge on its keel – known locally as 'fleetin'. Then, with sail set, they would return to land their cargoes ashore, often with the decks so heavily awash it looked as though only the sails were above the water. There is still one modern gravel barge working the estuary today.

On 12 January, 1899, a three-masted, full-rigged ship of 1900 tons, the *Forrest Hall*, was travelling in ballast, under tow from Bristol to Liverpool with a skeleton crew of 15 aboard. At mid-day the coastguards reported foul weather approaching from the Atlantic, which by late afternoon

Gravel barges on the Taw/Torridge estuary

had become the worst conditions experienced for many years. High winds, torrential rain and enormous seas swept the Bristol Channel, smashing houses in Ilfracombe, bringing the highest tide ever recorded on the river Avon, and flooding the port and railway station on the pier at Bristol.

The towing cable between the *Forrest Hall* and its tug, unable to take the strain of the pounding sea, broke leaving the *Forrest Hall* with her rudder useless, trailing two anchors and wallowing helplessly towards the North Devon coast off Porlock.

The Master of the *Forrest Hall*, Captain James Uliss, realised that his hope of salvation rested in the anchors taking firm hold on the bottom, allowing him to ride out the storm. But unable to depend on this, he sent up distress signals.

The rockets were seen at Porlock Weir and an urgent message was telegraphed to the nearest lifeboat station at Lynmouth; the last telegraph message dispatched that night before the gale blew down the lines.

Conditions in Lynmouth were atrocious. Mountainous seas were breaking over the jetty, roof-top high. If the lifeboat were launched here it would have to be into the belly of these waves. The situation was impossible.

The coxswain of the Lynmouth lifeboat, Jack Crocombe, realising he could not launch into Lynmouth harbour, nor send a warning to another lifeboat, made a momentous decision.

'We'll launch from Porlock,' he said, and so they did. Using a team of 18 horses hitched to the lifeboat carriage, they undertook an incredible 20-kilometre journey across Exmoor by road. Buffeted by wind and drenched by rain, climbing the terrifying one-in-four gradient rising 430

Rescue of the Forrest Hall (*Manuscript Ltd. Liskeard*)

metres up Countisbury Hill. At Ashton Gate, discovering the carriage was too wide for the narrow lane, they off-loaded the boat and sent the carriage on a circular route across the moor to wait ahead of them. They manoeuvred the lifeboat forward on wooden skids; every two metres the skids were dragged out, re-set and the boat pushed on over them again.

Pulling, pushing, twisting and turning, knocking down a garden wall, sawing down a large elm tree to facilitate their passage, they proceeded down the most dangerous hill in England leading into Porlock.

They did launch from Porlock and by 7 a.m. had helped the tug to secure another cable aboard *Forrest Hall*, and stood by her all the way to the Welsh coast and safe anchorage at Barry.

Skylark and black grouse

Exmoor National Park

Exmoor National Park is one of ten such parks throughout England and Wales – all places of outstanding beauty, containing large areas of wild countryside. Equally they are areas where the normal work of the countryside is daily carried on by farmers, foresters and horticulturists who play a vital role in providing the nation's food and timber. Exmoor National Park covers 686 square kilometres of farmland, forest, moorland and rugged cliff-tops that provide a perfect habitat for an abundance of animal and plant life. The purpose of all national parks is the protection of wildlife and the conservation and preservation of natural beauty, whilst at the same time providing facilities and access for the general public to enjoy open-air recreational activities. The Park is administered by the Exmoor National Park authority, which is responsible for controlling all development and industrial expansion within the area, protecting rights-of-way and providing caravan sites and car parks. They are also responsible for the route-markers on the Coast Path and other scheduled walks within the Park, and the alternative route just completed from Culbone to Wingate Combe is a splendid indication of their competence in this field. There is also a Park Warden service which I found most helpful and considerate. National parks are a vital part of our national heritage, preserving the landscape for future generations. However, at the same time, the normal professional working life and the domestic life of the countryside continues within the Park boundries and visitors should always remember that and follow the Country Code (see page 112).

Countisbury Church and across Exmoor

Minehead
to Porlock Weir
13½ kilometres

Map 1

It is written in the Domesday Book that, after dispossessing Edgar, Earl of Mercia, William the Conqueror gave what was known as Quay Town in Somerset to his friend William de Mohun of Dunster. Thus, from a contraction of Mohun and the Saxon *heved* (head) it has been suggested, Minehead took its name. A more likely suggestion, however, is that the name derives from the Welsh *mynydd* meaning mountain, for Minehead lies under a considerable hill that dominates the town and provides walkers with a foretaste of things to come on the Coast Path.

In bygone days Minehead consisted of three separate communities. *Higher Town* still retains a number of old thatched cottages with typically West Somerset abutting chimneys, and includes the much-photographed and painted passage-way known as Church Steps. *Lower or Middle Town* was eighteenth century and almost entirely destroyed by the Great Fire of Minehead in 1791, except for a row of almshouses in Market Lane. These were built in 1630 by merchant mariner Robert Quirke as a thanksgiving offering for the safe delivery of himself and his three-masted barque from a severe storm. And finally, *Quay Town* which includes the harbour.

The earliest mention of Quay Town harbour is for outstanding harbour dues in 1380. The Luttrell family owned the whole area and built a jetty during the fifteenth century, which was replaced by George Luttrell in 1616 with a pier to the west of the original. This was later extended by a succeeding member of the family and survives today. The harbour's most successful period was during the early 1700s when over 40 vessels were registered. A flourishing shipyard existed on the site of the present lifeboat station, and a busy trade was carried on between Ireland, the West Indies and Virginia. The last trading vessel registered here was the *Harriet*, a small sloop built in 1805 and smashed to pieces by a rising tide and on-shore gale whilst stranded on the beach after unloading lime in 1852. The Luttrell family finally sold the harbour to the Urban District Council for the sum of £2 in 1951. Today

Minehead

Above Grexy Combe

19

the harbour is only used by a handful of small fishing and pleasure boats, with occasional visits from the White Funnel Steamers operating from Swansea, Mumbles, Lynmouth and Clovelly, with cruises to Lundy Island.

An ancient ceremony associated with Quay Town, surviving from the Middle Ages and probably much earlier, is the Minehead Hobby Horse which appears every May Day accompanied by a drummer and an accordian player, prancing and dancing, swishing its long tail and swirling its elaborately decorated, brightly coloured houselling around in an effort to entice those ladies, as yet without child, under its skirt in order to rectify their barren state, as is the purpose of this fertility rite. Only one other town in Britain celebrates May Day with a Hobby Horse, and that also on this coast but further west, at Padstow in Cornwall.

Situated in an old cellar beneath a store on the harbour is the tiny Fishermen's chapel of St. Peter upon the Quay where regular services are still held. It's well worth a visit before returning to Quay Street.

Crossing the road and entering a narrow alley between old cottages, 90 metres west of the Red Lion Hotel, is the start of the Path from Minehead. It is signposted *Path to North Hill*, and a right turn following the acorn symbol leads up a flight of steps and then continues on a zig-zagging, climbing path uphill to the junction of Beacon Wood and Burgundy Road. Almost immediately the noises and smells of a traffic-clogged holiday resort are left behind as the Path, rising steeply from the pebbled Devonian sandstone beach – built up through centuries of westerly tides and gales – climbs towards the North Hill summit over 300 metres above sea-level. Here the fourteenth-century tower of Minehead's Parish Church of St. Michael stands sentinel over the Bristol Channel, giving assurance and comfort to passing mariners through-out the centuries.

Now the Path turns to the right and enters Culver Cliff Wood. At the Exmoor National Park boundary it veers off on to the left-hand track and continues along this route to the point where it starts to run down towards Green-aleigh Farm. Take another left fork here and continue walking above Greenaleigh Farm and Greenaleigh Sands – 180 metres below – as the Path leaves Culver Cliff Wood to enter Greenaleigh Plantation. There are a number of footpaths and tracks throughout these woods, all with inter-connecting routes running parallel at different levels, the top level being a bridleway. The Coast Path follows a middle course until Burgundy Combe where it takes a sharp left turn out of the woods to the broad landscape of Exmoor.

To this point the paths made in the last century by the Luttrells, who owned these woods and stocked them with

Pheasants, sycamore, and Scots pine beyond

pheasants, have wound their way through sycamore,
Scots pine, sessile oak, holly and rowan, which in
September illuminate the enclosing green and brown with
bright slashes of vivid red allowing, through the dense
foliage, occasional glimpses of the sea, which can be
heard surging and clattering amongst the boulders and
pebbles that frame Greenaleigh Sands beneath. Now the
Path emerges into open, purple-carpeted moorland with
unlimited views of the surrounding sea and landscape.

Immediately below, down a precipitous incline, midway
between Grexy Combe and Greenaleigh Farm, are the
remains of a small oblong building almost enshrouded in
briars, called Burgundy Chapel. No one seems to know
why. It could have been a votive chapel erected by a
soldier returning from the Burgundian wars as a token of
gratitude for his survival; or a haven of rest for the

occupants of Dunster Castle, as the household accounts for 1405 seem to suggest. Certainly a study of the remaining architecture is no help – a door-jamb with an indeterminate arch and a wall about a metre high and two metres long. There is an alternative path to the chapel which can be joined at Quay West in Minehead, passing the harbour and gasworks to Greenaleigh Farm, through the farmyard, along a level path for 800 metres to the foot of the combe. My advice, however, if you are walking the Coast Path to Porlock Weir, is not to venture down and obviously have to climb back up again – the effort involved is far greater than the aesthetic or spiritual rewards.

Follow the course of the combe up to the left, away from the chapel and, at the top, turn right past Bramble Combe inside a bank and fence protecting cultivated farm fields. Soon Grexy Combe appears on the right. A short distance from the Path down the combe to the left is Furzebury Brake, an Iron Age circular hill slip enclosure. It had an outer ditch that can still be traced in parts and a stone rampart. To visit it means crossing the stream that once supplied the occupants with their water.

Left again, and nearer the Path, are the ruins of East Myne farmhouse; further along a road leads down to West Myne ruins. This is easy going now with springy turf underfoot and soon, rising ahead, is Selworthy Beacon. A deviation from the Coast Path to enjoy the view from this summit is very simple to undertake, and thoroughly rewarding.

Beneath the Beacon lies the village of Selworthy, thought by many to be the most beautiful village in England. Its seven delightful thatched cottages climb the lane to a wooded mound where the open door of the white-painted Selworthy church discloses a view as fair as any in the land, looking far out over Porlock Vale to the hills and combes of Exmoor. The church tower is fourteenth century, as is the chancel. The south aisle, rebuilt in 1490, is considered a treasure of English church architecture. The church contains a chained book of 1609, *A Defence of Bishop Jewel's Apology of the Church of England* and, on the wall, a notice concerning the Oath of Allegiance sent by King James I to all churches in England. In the year 1052 the lady of the manor of Selworthy was Eadgyth, sister of King Harold. Today's lord of the manor is the National Trust.

On the south-eastern spur between Selworthy village and the Beacon is situated Bury Castle – another Iron Age hill slope enclosure, bigger than Furzebury Brake. The outside ditch encloses an area of 1½ hectares and an inner earth work, over two metres high, surrounds half-a-hectare. Above Bury Castle, near a disused quarry track, is a stone hut marked on the Ordnance Survey map and described on its memorial stone as a *wind and weather hut.*

It was erected to the memory of Sir Thomas Dyke Acland (1787–1871) who it is said walked to this spot every Sunday morning with his children, talking to them of life, the beauty of this Exmoor countryside, and trying to instil in them some of his own love of poetry.

Leaving Selworthy Beacon, the Coast Path approaches Bossington Hill on the left, where a raised crown of stones announces that the Exmoor National Park authority has given permission for hang-gliding to take place from this hill. Participants launch themselves from 250 metres at a point between the summit and Hurlstone Point to soar and sail over Bossington Beach and Porlock Bay imitating the actions of the gulls that frequent the secluded ledges of the cliffs. The Point can be approached along an alternative route slightly lower down, dangerous in places, but with breathtaking panoramic views of North Somerset, Devon and, on a clear bright day, across the Channel to Wales.

Westward the spectacular wooded cliffs of Porlock, Porlock Weir and Ashley Combe reach up to join with those of Glenthorne, and on to Foreland Point, rising 230 metres sheer out of the sea to meet them. Inland, across the bare uplands of central Exmoor, the large mass of Dunkery Beacon and the Brendon Hills can be seen. Seawards a continuous flow of small fishing boats and pleasure craft criss-cross wakes, sailing from Minehead, Porlock, Lynton, Ilfracombe and Clovelly, whilst larger and more stately vessels – coasters and container ships – steam between the ports of Swansea, Cardiff, Newport, Bristol and also Watchet. The Welsh coastline, from Porthcawl to Penarth, is exposed to view, marred only by the cruel white of Margam steel foundry.

Pause here, rest and catch breath; absorb the view and enjoy it before continuing on past the coastguard look-out to rejoin the Path as it makes a steep descent down Hurlstone Combe to where the National Trust signpost reads *Bossington to Huntstone Point*, and follow the path towards Bossington.

Huntstone is a variant of Hurlstone, probably the more ancient name, which helps to perpetuate the local legend, recounted by John Lloyd Warden Page in *The Coast of Devon:*

'The amiable Giant of Grabbist Wood close by Dunster chose this point to challenge the Devil to a game of quoits using boulders. The Devil, finding himself out-thrown but only just, cheated; whereupon the Giant picked him up by the tail and threw him into the Bristol Channel.'

On the motor road from Lynton to Porlock, at its highest point near where the road from Exford descends to join it, are two massive stones known as the Whit Stones. These are the hurled stones of the legend.

Continue along the Path towards Bossington until it runs upstream alongside the bank of the river Horner for a short distance before turning right over the footbridge into Bossington car park.

The village of Bossington is one of those Exmoor villages and hamlets that time seems to have passed by. Situated on the Holnicote Estate, which belongs to the National Trust, the thatched roofs of its cottages are supported by ancient walls of tremendous thickness carrying quaint round chimneys, which look decorative but are also decidedly functional. Joined to Bossington is the tiny hamlet of Lynch with a medieval Chapel of Ease.

There are two ways of leaving Bossington; a path beginning just beyond Lower House leads across fields to Porlock, where there are a number of hotels, restaurants and cafés. You can see the wood-shingled spire of the church of St. Dubricius, a fifth-century Welsh saint who is alleged to have crowned King Arthur and officiated at his wedding to Guinevere, and who is buried in Llandaff Cathedral.

The Coast Path continues past the car park, turning right again and following the sign marked *Bossington Beach*. From here it follows red waymarks leading past the ruins of two old lime-kilns, along a wide track obviously used by lorries, and climbing three successive stiles, laid out ahead of each other like hurdles across marshy fields behind the pebble ridge marking the sea-line boundary of the lush Vale of Porlock. Here the marshes and fields produce abundant pasture and barley for which the region is famous. This is probably due to currents of warm damp air funnelled in through the north-facing towering heights encircling Porlock from Hurlstone to Gore Points, making this the most fertile area in the whole National Park. The reed beds of these marshes provide a winter haunt for migrant birds – winter duck, mallard, teal, wigeon, shovellers, waders on autumn passage, also green sand-pipers, ringed plovers and greenshanks. Many years ago this Bay of Porlock held very productive oyster beds. Today, alas, only the industrious oyster-catcher displays an interest in searching for this succulent bivalve, and the harvest of the sea is predominantly plastic jetsam washed ashore from mid-channel dumping grounds.

The Coast Path leaves the track and takes to the large pebbles and boulders of the beach; this is heavy going, so keep close to the sea-wall where there are flat stretches of grass and sand until you can climb the stone steps leading to Porlock main road, and turn right into Porlock Weir.

Porlock Weir was a herring port up to the eighteenth century. During the nineteenth century the port entrance was improved to take vessels of 12-foot draught bringing limestone, coal, sand and cement and taking away the produce of the Vale and, during the war, pit props for

24

Medieval Chapel of Ease, Bossington

South Wales. It is a difficult harbour to negotiate, with broom beacons to port and stick beacons to starboard, and a lock gate opened at low tide to flush out the channel. It is used nowadays by yachtsmen and local angling boats.

The Ship Inn has served this Exmoor community for possibly 900 years, and beams have been uncovered suggesting that a great deal of its woodwork came from the deckhead timbers of wrecked vessels. Here – soaked to the skin, after a perambulation across Exmoor – the poet Southey wrote a (not very good) 'thank you' sonnet for the inn's hospitality as he dried out in its fire-warmed chimney corner:

'Here by the unwelcome summer rain confined;
But often shall hereafter call to mind . . .'

This tiny harbour is well-blessed, possessing not only the Ship Inn but also the Anchor Hotel.

Hang gliding over Bossington

Porlock Weir
to Lynmouth

17 kilometres Maps 2 – 3

On leaving Porlock Weir there are two paths available: one signposted behind the Anchor Hotel through a gate past the stables; the other, round the front of the hotel, climbs steps on the left. Both paths, however, meet after a short distance in a meadow above the harbour, and proceed together through pleasant fields before taking to the road for a short distance on approaching Worthy Lodge. Here motorists, on payment of a small toll, may drive the delightful wooded road that avoids notorious Porlock Hill bringing them out on the A39 between Porlock and County Gate. Walkers may pass – without charge – through the white gate on the right, crossing Worthy Combe, entering Ashley Combe, then the dark, brooding grandeur of Yearnor Woods, which cling to the steep slopes leading to the tiny church at Culbone. For over three kilometres the Path climbs upwards under a leafy canopy, at times so dense the sunlight scarcely illuminates the path beneath.

During the year 1265 these woods, known then as Kitnor, were inhabited by whole families – outcasts of society, offenders against church or state – banished here to live lonely, isolated lives without dwelling places or provisions. Forbidden to leave or establish contact with the world outside, they somehow survived 40 years before the last one died. Again, in 1385 for 100 years, Kitnor was used as a prison colony until other methods of punishment were devised. The woods were then left as nature fashioned them until 1544 when the authorities decided to use Kitnor as a site for a leper colony. Forty-five men, women and children – all lepers – were sent here, again without help of any kind, and they somehow survived for 78 years before the last leper died in 1622.

Some time after the year 1720 the unlikeliest colony of all arrived in these woods. Thirty-eight East Indian prisoners of war, captured during the British conquest of India, were sent to Kitnor (then becoming known as Culbone) to work as charcoal burners. After 21 years they were allowed to leave and their places were taken by local men eager to carry on the profession which, by this time, had established a flourishing trade across the Channel to

'Pill box' from second world war, Porlock Weir

Wales. The ruins of the stone dwellings lived in by these men, their burning pits alongside the many swift-flowing streams falling steeply to the sea, the paths they trod through the heavily-wooded area between Culbone and Glenthorne, can still be traced; as can evidence of another once-prosperous woodland industry, oak felling. Thousands of tonnes of this timber, cut into planks – in still visible saw-pits – left here for the flourishing ship-builders of the South West.

Culbone Church stands almost at the summit of the woodland climb. Reckoned to be the smallest complete church in England it must surely be the only church mentioned in both Domesday and the Guinness Book of Records. The Path* runs alongside the church wall past the small gate into the churchyard, then climbs away past red signposted route markers towards Silcombe through Withycombe Wood. Emerging from the wood at a gate having on one side a metal, two-tread mounting block with built-in boot-scraper (obviously for the benefit of returning huntsmen rather than dedicated walkers) take to the tarmac road where the Path sweeps round to the right climbing gently past Silcombe Farm, Halmer and Twitchen Combes, around Holmes Combe – where track and roadway meet at crossroads which are signposted. The Path passes the yard of Broomstreet Farm to climb again for one kilometre along a track high-banked and hedged, denying a glimpse of sea on the right. Rising steeply to the heights of Yenworthy Common, the Path crosses the spring-fed waters that rise above Guskin and Eastmead Linhays to arrive at Yenworthy Farm. The path leading to the track passing the front of the farmhouse is signposted *County*

* *There is an alternative route between Culbone and Wingate Combe (see page 33).*

Gate via Gt. Yenworthy Farm, and points across the centre of a steeply sloping large field which, on the last occasion I walked it, had been recently ploughed and seeded allowing no access for walkers to the limits of the field verges. The extremely helpful Park Warden at County Gate informed me that this was part of extensive Exmoor farmland reclamation, but assured me that – seeded or unseeded – the Coast Path went across the centre of the field and that is where you must go. When a farmer ploughs over the track in this way, he has six weeks grace in which to restore the Path.

On a track leading down to Yenworthy from the main road are a large number of stone cairns, often described locally as the burial mounds of the Doones (for more about the Doones, see page 106).

The Path now follows the farm road for 800 metres, turning sharp right on the route for County Gate just before the buildings of Yenworthy Lodge, and making its way across high open moorland to County Gate and the Devon/Somerset border.

At County Gate is an Exmoor National Park information centre and a car park. The Path crosses the county boundary over the A39 on Cosgate Hill. From its summit the whole of the legendary Doone Country can be viewed, with Badgworthy Water (pronounced 'Badgery') making its journey past Great Black Hill and Cloud Hill running on to join the Oare water at Malmsmead, and together they continue as the East Lyn river (uniting with the waters of Hoaroak and Farley at Waters Meet) to Lynmouth. At the entrance to Ashton Farm, on the left, the Path emerges onto a grassy strip. Follow the roadside for about 300 metres before turning right across the road through Wingate and along the side of Old Barrow Hill with its circular Roman signal station high above. Making a steep descent down Wingate Combe the Path – now well indicated by acorn-marked trees – levels out through Wingate Wood* emerging on cliffs above a distinctive tree-covered island in the sea off Desolate Point – known as Sir Robert's Chair. It is named after Sir Robert Chichester who was shot at Crowcombe Barton, near Lynton, and in various forms, including driving a flaming coach up and down the cliffs, is said to haunt this area to such effect that the local people prevailed upon the rector of Bratton Fleming to try and exorcize his malignant presence.

Having returned to the coastline the Path follows it closely for nearly three kilometres through the coppiced oaks of Kipscombe Enclosure, crossing Kipscombe Combe to join the road that leads to Foreland Lighthouse. Stay with the road to Caddow Combe where the signpost, pointing inland, reads *Countisbury 1½ miles* and, in the

* *The alternative route rejoins the main Path here.*

Foreland Point lighthouse

other direction, *Lighthouse*, indicating a right-of-way to
Foreland Point and the lighthouse – an experience I
heartily recommend – before picking up the Path again.
Travel down hill for a short distance until reaching a stone
shed. The Path then climbs steeply over scree and grassland leaving the Foreland on the right and approaching
Great Red – a deep gully north of Blackhead Point. This
forms the meeting place of predominantly sandstone Foreland grits which we have walked over from Minehead, with
the slaty rocks of the Lynton Beds ahead of us – all being
of the Lower Devonian geological period. You pass two

signposts indicating the route to the left alongside Butter Hill. This provides another magnificent view of the North Devon coast, Lynton and Lynmouth to the Valley of Rocks down to the gold of Sillery Sands – 270 metres below.

Almost by the churchyard of St. John the Baptist, Countisbury, the Path turns sharp right descending Countisbury Hill. It is an opportunity to cross the road and take refreshment in the Blue Ball Inn before visiting the site of a most famous victory over the Danes in 878 during the reign of King Alfred. Countisbury Castle is an Iron Age promontory fortress guarding Wind Hill and so constructed as to be unassailable on two sides due to the steepness of the hill. It was defended by a deep ditch and enormous rampart nearly ten metres high crowned with a palisade. But it had one fault – there was no fresh water supply. This fact was known to Hubba, the Dane, who led 23 vessels across from Wales to land on the Exmoor coast against the defending forces of Odun, the ealderman of Devon. Hubba prepared to wait – confident of success. The defenders – reversing roles – became the attackers, quitting the castle and rushing down the hillside to annihilate Hubba and 800 of his men.

On leaving the castle an alternative, and more interesting, route is signposted. It leads from above the inn through the grandeur of open moorland into the seclusion of woods and clear-running streams, tumbling over boulder-strewn channels, towards the breathtaking spectacle of Watersmeet; and after descending through moorland again, round Summerhouse Hill to the West Lyn at Lynbridge, finally takes to the road to enter Lynmouth.

The Coast Path follows the A39, but at a slightly lower level to a point opposite the Beacon Hotel, where it takes to the road for 180 metres before turning off to the right. The Path then passes through woods leading down a zig-zag track to the beach behind the Holiday Fellowship's Manor House.

Odun captures the Danish standard

31

An alternative route: Culbone to Wingate Combe

7½ kilometres

Map 2

This alternative route was introduced in 1979 and is, without doubt, a most exciting and beautiful addition to the Coast Path between Culbone and Wingate Combe. But it should not be walked alone except by experienced walkers equipped with adequate boots and rucksack containing items suitable for emergency use (see page 2) including food and drink. For until reaching Countisbury there is absolutely nowhere this can be obtained, and it is most unlikely any other person will be met with or seen for at least seven kilometres.

Having written this, however, let me stress that the benefits derived from undertaking this route are immense. The path hugs the coastline all the way – albeit at a considerable height above the sea for long stretches – winding and twisting, climbing and descending through thickly-growing oaks, sycamore, rowan, holly, an abundance of sweet chestnut, conifer and rhododendron. Here and there can be seen glimpses of the Channel across to Wales, always to the music of falling streams, bird song, the eternal cry of gulls, the plaintive high-pitched call of sailing buzzards and the surging channel tide on the boulder-scattered beaches beneath.

The alternative route follows the Coast Path from Porlock Weir to Culbone, where it crosses the churchyard. Here the Exmoor National Park signposts display yellow and blue symbols – blue for the alternative path. This turns to the left around the side of Knap Tor before descending – gently at first – on a carpet of fallen oak leaves through Culbone Wood, crossing Silcombe stream, turning sharply left and right through Twitchen Combe, with a very steep descent and ascent on each side. All the way the route is adequately marked with blue-blazed trees and signposts indicating diversions, often to well-made steps avoiding the old foresters' tracks which have become dangerous, and for this reason have been blocked off with felled trees.

Culbone Church

33

Scots pine

Corsican pine

Monterey cypress

European larch

Another difficult twisting and turning section leads to Broomstreet Combe and on to Embelle Wood. Then it is fairly easy going to Yenworthy Wood where the path snakes around and under Sugarloaf Hill past a sign marked *Guildhall Corner*, the name given to the imposing rock face that can be seen from Sugarloaf Hill. Now the path leaves Yenworthy Wood running along the fringe of Stags Head Wood to enter Glenthorne Estate.

The Reverend Walter Stephen Halliday established this estate in 1830 when he built Glenthorne House, although the last major addition to the house was not completed until 1846. Designed during the heyday of the Romantic Movement it is 'Tudoresque' in style. But most of Glenthorne's visitors come not for the architecture, but for the splendour of the woods which contain many rare trees.

Previous to Halliday's occupation, the cliffs around the house were bare or covered with scrub, due probably to the ravages of a large flock of feral goats which roamed the woods between here and Culbone. Halliday planted sheltering rows of Monterey cypress and then, in the combes bordering the five-kilometre driveway, introduced beech, larch, Scots pine and Corsican pine. He then turned his attention to the equally ravaged Stags Head and Yenworthy Woods. In a sheltered combe he established a pinetum which includes Grecian pine, Morinda spruce and many other mature specimens over 30 metres high, and one particular Wellingtonia of 37 metres.

The alternative path runs above the pinetum through Steeple Stuart new plantation. (Once grass fields cultivated by mule, they have been recently planted with drifts of different varieties of conifer.) The route crosses Coscombe where the stream marks the border between Devon and Somerset, and the dense thickets provide ample cover for the deer which flourish in the woods.

Immediately after leaving the combe, to the right of the path is a large stone known as Decision Stone. Here Halliday sat whilst deciding whether or not he should make his home at Glenthorne, and afterwards he recorded the date on the stone. The spring, covered by a stone dome with a granite cross bolted through the centre on top of it, has water emerging through a marble trough brought from Greece. It was built by Halliday who christened it Sisters Fountain in honour of his sisters. The decorative copse of pines that once sheltered the fountain has completely weathered away and is being replaced by noble fir – one of the hardiest of all conifers.

The path leaves the fountain through Glenthorne Plantation climbing to Tapler Ridge with signposts leading through wooden gates, and a splendid view of the house and beach 400 metres below. Coal and lime were once shipped direct from South Wales and landed on this beach, and the remains of the old lime-kilns and boathouse can still be seen. And almost immediately beneath, at the

Smugglers landing a cargo

meeting place of the two streams, is the mud wallow made by the red deer which, during the October rutting season, is enlivened by the sight and sound of stags rolling in it.

Passing between gate-posts, surmounted by sculptured boars' heads, the path turns sharp left away from the lodge to turn once again parallel with the coast along a route called Brandy Path that, in the eighteenth century, had the more forbidding title of Horror Shade. This whole estate is a maze of paths and tracks put to good use throughout the centuries. Smuggling flourished along this channel, and for some time Glenthorne was its centre.

This final stretch of path to Wingate Combe is sheer delight. You frequently emerge from a dense tunnel of rhododendrons to find that the cliff drops sheer away to the sea beneath, allowing uninterrupted views of the coastline to east and west and across the channel to Wales. Gulls and cormorants cover the cliff ledges and small rock islands, and buzzards soar on the salt updraught. Kestrels hover over cliff edge gorse and bracken, and ill-mannered jays, constantly disturbed, fly angrily ahead. Occasionally, on the left, appear small, stone-built round shelters used as look-outs – often by smugglers. Finally the route leaves Brandy Path, taking to the bracken leading down towards the sea at Wingate Combe, and the two coast paths become one acorn-signed path making towards Foreland Point and Lynton.

It is possible to visit Glenthorne without walking the Coast Path. There is a nature trail to Glenthorne beach covering a distance of five kilometres around the estate including every aspect of its development and beauty. It can be approached from County Gate; a written guide is available. Exmoor National Park issue a pamphlet of suggested walks around Glenthorne Estate, obtainable from the County Gate centre.

Barn owl

Lynmouth
to Combe Martin

21 kilometres   Maps 3 – 4

The Coast Path from Lynmouth starts from the beach path, crosses the footbridges of the Lyn, turning right along Riverside Road and passing the harbour with its famous Rhenish tower which – in common with most of the surrounding buildings – has been rebuilt after the tragic flooding in 1952.

Heavy rain had fallen on Exmoor for two weeks prior to the flooding. The large expanse of level moorland, 500 metres above sea-level and consisting solely of blanket bog supporting deer sedge – known as The Chains – which supplies the waters of the Barle, Exe, West Lyn and Hoaroak, had reached saturation point when, in five disastrous hours of concentrated fury, it is estimated a further 3,200 million gallons of water descended upon it. Below the hill peat of The Chains is a soil layer of no more than 100 millimetres and beneath that a hard thin crust known as the 'iron pan', forming an impermeable barrier through which no water drains. Every gallon of water falling that night ran off The Chains through steep-sided combes leading into gullies dropping precipitously down towards Lynmouth where, finally, the East and West Lyn rivers (swollen into torrents), joined together and swept down upon the helpless port. The flood carried rocks and boulders (some weighing ten tonnes), up-rooted trees, tore down bridges, knocked down houses, and finally the Rhenish tower, as the water, released from containment, spread out over the harbour sweeping cars and boats before it.

The many true stories of tragedy and heroism that night will never be known, but the resulting loss of life and the material damage aroused the nation into instant response, and the disaster fund was generously supported. This enabled the authorities quickly and efficiently to rebuild Lynmouth without affecting its picturesque quality or popularity as a holiday resort. The improvements made during the rebuilding to ensure against such an event happening again have proved successful. Every effort was made to restore the area to its original architectural style, including building a new Rhenish tower, although

37

Flood-damaged Lynmouth 1952

why this structure – built in 1850 by General Rawdon – has this name is unknown. It bears little resemblance to a Rhineland tower and it is believed the design was copied from a painting Rawdon saw in the house of a friend.

Leave Lynmouth from Riverside Road with the tower on the right, crossing the road to turn left by the pavilion on a metalled path signposted *To the Valley of Rocks*, which winds uphill to join the path to the north of Hollerday Hill called North Walk – a path cut to the Valley of Rocks by a Mr. Sanford in 1817.

Another way of reaching the Valley of Rocks from Lynmouth is to use the fascinating Cliff Railway, built in 1890 at a cost of £8,000. It is gravity-driven, a tank beneath the rail car at the top of the line being filled with three tonnes of water which, on descending, pulls up the bottom car by means of an endless cable. The tank is emptied at the bottom whilst the tank at the top is refilled. When first operated it had the steepest gradient of any railway in the world – more than one-in-four rising up to a height of 140 metres along a 900-metre track. The railway was given to the town by Sir George Newnes, the publisher, who lived in Lynton for many years. The footpath up from Lynmouth crosses and re-crosses this line three times before reaching North Walk.

On leaving the cliff railway rejoin the Path at North Walk. There is another route out of Lynton which takes

38

you into the town from the railway, passing the Town Hall on the right, into the public grounds on Hollerday Hill. As the Path climbs, veering away to the left, you will see a signpost reading *Higher Path*. Follow this to come out high above North Walk looking down and ahead at the Valley of Rocks.

The North Walk to the Valley of Rocks was a favourite walk of the poet Shelley, who spent his honeymoon with sixteen-year-old Harriet Westbrook in a Lynmouth cottage owned by a Miss Hooper. During the nine weeks he spent here he wrote *Queen Mab*.

Although only 1½ kilometres in length North Walk is a brilliant feat of engineering. It is also of superb scenic beauty commanding splendid views of the Welsh coast with the path at times dropping sheer away to the sea pounding below; climbing round and above lichen-covered rocks and boulders, the orange, umber and grey colouring broken by dark patches of ground ivy; twisting and turning until running down between the rock masses of Ragged Jack and Castle Rock, their fortress-like, castellated towers guarding the entrance to the Valley of Rocks.

The Valley, as far as can be determined, was created during the Ice Age 10,000 years ago. Then, a sheet of ice covered the area of sea around Cornwall and Devon, and pressed tight against this high cliffed coastline. This forced back the rivers seeking access to the sea and caused them to find alternative drainage routes along the verges of the ice; often, like this valley, running parallel with the coast. As the ice retreated it deposited glacial till (a mixture of clay with boulders). We are on the slate rocks of the Lower or Middle Devonian period known as the Lynton Beds, which change in the Woody Bay area to the predominantly sandstone rock of the Hangman Grits, returning to slate again with the Ilfracombe Beds and Morte Beds farther west.

Passing left of Castle Rock (although there is an exciting path to the top of Castle Rock) an alternative path leads down to the far end of the valley providing splendid opportunities for seeing the herd of wild goats that have ranged free here for centuries. The Coast Path proper takes to the road, passing on the left the track up to Mother Meldrun's cave (see page 107).

Continue now along the toll road past Lee Abbey – once Ley Manor. It never was an abbey but was the seat of the de Wichehalse family from 1628 to 1730. The present house was built on the site of Ley Manor in 1841 by Charles Bailey and was bought by the Anglicans in 1945 to be turned into the Lee Abbey Community, one of the largest mixed religious communities in Europe. Within the grounds of this estate is Duty Point, above Wringcliff Bay. Here stands an ivy-covered folly close to the precipice known as Jennifred's Leap, named (it is alleged) after

Jennifred de Wichehalse. During the reign of James II (1685–1688) she was courted by Lord Auberley but, having achieved the object of his desire, he deserted her. Unable to take the shame of her actions, Jennifred threw herself from the top of the cliff. Her father complained to the king – a good friend of Lord Auberley – who did nothing. During the Monmouth Rebellion de Wichehalse joined the rebels and, at Sedgemoor, revenged his daughter's honour by meeting her betrayer face-to-face and slaying him in battle. In cold fact there never was a Jennifred or Lord Auberley, and the house was eventually sold to pay off the family debts, after the family had moved to Chard. Unfortunately, the coast walk is not accessible at this point as it is on private property, although Lee Bay is accessible by a right of way from the road near Lower Lodge. At Lee Bay the cliffs are composed of formations of finely-layered metamorphic rock, rent and split by the intense heat and immense pressure that went into their creation. They are much explored by geologists interested in the quantities of quartz and mica they contain – as are the equally sundered dark slate and shale rocks of Wringcliff Bay to the east.

The Coast Path stays on the road, entering Crock Woods opposite Crock Point – making the only break in this continuous hogs-back coastal landscape. Here, during the eighteenth century, what is known as the 'Crock Pits clay' was worked and shipped to Holland, where it was much sought after by Dutch craftsmen for the fineness of its quality. Leaving Crock Woods to enter The Pines the Path reaches Woody Bay. There is a rather handsome alternative route to Woody Bay (see map 3). It starts opposite the entrance to Lee Abbey along a track, through a white gate with yellow, way-marked signs reading *Woodland walk leading to Woody Bay*, following through Crock and Croscombe Woods – and eventually The Pines – and crosses over two fairly new bridges with fine views of Lee and Woody Bays. Soon the path once again rejoins the tarmac road down to the Woody Bay Hotel.

Still on the tarmac road the Coast Path leaves the hotel, passing the car park, and then climbs steeply and doubles back to the left. In front is a gate marked with a National Park sign reading *To Hunter's Inn*. This is obviously a vehicle track and makes easy walking to Heddon's Mouth providing one of the finest sections of this coast walk. Passing first through West Woody Bay Woods, teeming with wildlife – rabbits and squirrels constantly crossing the path ahead, buzzards and kestrels soaring and hovering above, the Coast Path then leaves the woods, turns inland and crosses Hollow Brook Combe. Turning seaward around Martinhoe Beacon, the Coast Path crosses the site of the second Roman signal station occupied between A.D. 50 and A.D. 70, by about 60 Roman soldiers who took over this

Lee Bay

fortification after abandoning Old Barrow station above Glenthorne in A.D. 54.

Here, between the splendour of the aptly-named Cow and Calf coastline and the Beacon, the rock structure changes again from the Lynton Beds to Hangman Grits making the composition of Highveer Point. The Point rises sheer in gorse, heather and scree-covered slopes to 213 metres – its rugged grandeur and isolation creating an eastern bastion for Heddon's Mouth – plunging down a gradient of seven-in-ten to the pebble and boulder-covered beach with its lonely lime-kiln ruin.

Finally, after passing around Hill Brook, the Coast Path – now with fine views along the densely-wooded Heddon Valley towards Heale Down and South Down, Parracombe and across to the great mass of Heddon's Mouth Cleave – drops down through Road Wood to Hunter's Inn. Here you can rest and prepare for the climb to come.

Before leaving Hunter's Inn I must mention a walk missed by travelling the cliff top route from Woody Bay to here. But this path should only be attempted by experienced walkers, suitably clad, and should never be travelled alone (see map 3).

It begins beside the Woody Bay Hotel down a path signposted *Woody Bay Beach*. Turning left at the bottom and carrying on until reaching a junction left and right, it takes the much wider right-hand path, passing over a stile before the route becomes narrower again and overhung with brambles, nettles, shrubs and bushes, emerging

42

finally to witness the glories of Hollow Brook waterfall, formed by a stream rising near Martinhoe and plummeting down to the sea – barely 800 metres away from its source – through a series of falls, the largest cascading over a ridge across the path to disappear to the beach 70 metres below between the boulders of a narrow gorge running to the sea. The beauty of this sight compensates for the effort involved in reaching it. From here the path continues in equal splendour to Highveer Point entering the Heddon Valley beneath the Coast Path. You can either follow the Coast Path back to Hunter's Inn or drop down to the right to the beach at Heddon's Mouth, crossing the water by means of stepping stones or the wooden bridge and following a path from the lime-kiln to where it turns sharp right to climb a steep, zig-zag route through bracken to join the official Path by a signpost near the wall enclosing the fields above Heddon's Mouth Cleave.

From Hunter's Inn the Coast Path takes the Combe Martin road for 180 metres, past Trentishoe Combe Cottage on the right before climbing and turning off at a signpost reading *Coast Path to Combe Martin* to the right, and *Trentishoe Church*, to the left.

The church of St. Peter's, Trentishoe, partly rebuilt in 1861, stands in a lonely, sheltered valley within the sound of the sea. Inside it still retains a musicians' gallery, built in 1771, with a hole cut out of the woodwork to allow the bow of the bass viol to pass to and fro. Carved into this gallery is a neck of corn, marking a custom carried out for centuries on Devon farms, whereby the first sheaf of corn cut at harvest was carried back to the barn by the youngest man present whilst the others tried to throw water over it. If they succeeded it would be a wet harvest, if not, dry.

The Path from above Heddon's Mouth Cleave follows a stone wall above East Cleave, South Dean Corner and North Cleave, crossing two stiles. At one stage it runs along a narrow corridor formed by a wire fence on the left protecting sheep pasture, and a similar fence on the right safe-guarding the walker from the creeping danger of coastal erosion. All the time the Path is well signposted. You may, as I did one September, see a field white with mushrooms before skirting Neck Wood Gut and travelling across the open moor of Trentishoe Down to reach a sign pointing inland to a National Trust car park. Here the official Path turns right on the tarmac road for 180 metres before turning right again past a bungalow on to Holdstone Down. However, a vehicle-wide swathe, cut through purple ling, crosses Holdstone Down from the signpost in the direction of Sherrycombe providing ideal walking conditions. This moorland is owned by the National Trust. Eventually you arrive at a point above Sherrycombe, which is reached by turning left to climb past an acorn-marked signpost, then a slate set in the ground with a

Great Hangman

white-painted acorn; and in front another signpost indicating the route back to County Road or forward over a stile to make the very steep descent down to Sherrycombe.

Sherrycombe has a spectacular waterfall dropping from the cliff to the beach, but only an experienced climber would be capable of clambering down to view it. The exceedingly steep path, through bracken and brambles down to the wooden footbridge across the stream, will be difficult enough for most walkers, particularly as they have the much steeper and higher climb still to make up the other side to Girt Down and on to Great Hangman.

Great Hangman, viewed from Holdstone during late afternoon on a warm autumn day, with the sun creeping and dipping westward casting long shadows, throwing its summit into black relief against the heat haze, creates an atmosphere of deep foreboding. Great Hangman seems to have a brooding contempt for all mortals foolish enough to try and conquer its eastern wall. But conquered it must be before rest and refreshment can be obtained in Combe Martin.

The Path twists and turns, lessening the gradient – one-in-three in places – rising over Girt Down and becoming easier. It passes a signpost indicating Blackstone Point which, if you have the energy, provides a magnificent viewpoint for watching the colonies of birds inhabiting these cliffs – razorbills, guillemots, fulmars, cormorants, herring gulls, greater and lesser black-backed gulls, jackdaws and sometimes ravens. The cliff wall to the west of Great Hangman Gut, below the summit, rises

44

sheer to 250 metres and is perhaps the highest sea cliff in the South West.

Descending from the summit is relatively simple, starting from a signpost by a boundary wall leading to Little Hangman, where once again a slight diversion will provide magnificent views down to Wild Pear Beach below and ahead to Watermouth. Finally, the Path becomes a narrow lane – bordered by blackthorn and brambles – passing a number of houses, to run out into the car park at Combe Martin almost alongside the Exmoor National Park caravan on the left. From now on we leave the National Park behind.

Jackdaw, raven, and jay

Oyster catchers

Shovellers

Wigeon

Mallard

Teal

Greenshank

Ringed plover

Combe Martin
to Saunton Sands

20 kilometres

The village of Combe Martin is strung out along the valley of the river Umber. It is cut into two sections by the main road from Ilfracombe which, beginning at Seaside changes its name five times in less than two kilometres, to Borough Road, King Street, High Street, Castle Street and Victoria Street, before running out towards Blackmore Gate. The village is dominated by the parish church of St. Peter ad Vincula, built in the Early English and Perpendicular styles and probably dating back to 1200. It is connected with the churches of nearby Berrynarbor (see page 105) and that of Hartland in a North Devon folk song:

'Hartland for length
Berrynarbor for strength
Combe Martin for beauty.'

The Phoenicians may have come here to trade for silver and lead. Certainly the silver mines were operating during the reign of Edward I (1272–1307), worked by 337 miners brought down from the Peak District of Derbyshire. It is generally accepted that Combe Martin silver paid for the English victories at Cressy, Poitiers and Agincourt. The mines closed down in about 1848 being no longer economical to work.

To visit the mines from the beach, walk up King Street until it becomes High Street. On the right is an extraordinary example of hotel architecture *The Pack of Cards*, so-called because of a seventeenth-century gambler, George Ley, who won a considerable sum of money at cards and built the house to commemorate the event. It was built in the same manner that a child builds a house with playing cards, having four floors representing four suits; each floor with 13 doors for the 13 cards in each suit, and the whole building having 52 windows representing the number of cards in a pack. A large table may be seen in the passage, the top of which is cleverly hinged to lift up and allow two men lying full-length to hide inside, and thus, in more unpleasant days, escape the press gang, which forced local fishermen into the Royal

47

Navy. The route to the mines is opposite *The Pack of Cards*, on the left along Chapple Lane, into Wakeny Lane, over crossroads at Netherton Cross and straight ahead to the mines.

Leave Combe Martin on the Coast Path at the acorn sign along Berry Lane – a short walk that avoids the main road and passes fishermen's cottages. Continue out on the tarmac road again until reaching the Sandy Bay Hotel when the Path turns right and takes to the coast around Napps Hill. It is a pleasant walk past Golden Cove, through the fringes of Bamants Wood, past Small Mouth above Briery Cave, which is well worth a visit. Before the Path returns to the main road it reaches the inlet to Watermouth Bay, almost opposite Watermouth Castle. Watermouth Castle is a large house built in 1825. It may have been built upon earlier foundations for there is reason to believe it was the site of a battlemented castle in the fourteenth century. Today it houses an arts and crafts centre, and its seven hectares of grounds include terraced gardens with sub-tropical trees and shrubs and charming woodland walks.

Turn right into Widmouth Bay and *if the tide is out*, keep to the left along the rocky foreshore for about 80 metres where a set of steps take you up the pleasant wooded embankment to join the path. *If the tide is in*, continue along the road with caution for about 140 metres where you join the same path on top of the embankment via an access through the wall. (When walking in the opposite direction the state of the tide can be seen here and you can decide which route to take.) Continue along the pleasant wooded embankment towards Widmouth Head. Unfortunately, negotiations to continue the Path around Widmouth Head were not finalised at the time of going to press; until this is resolved the Path comes back onto the road until you turn right off the road at Samson's Bay. The Path then continues down around Rillage Point and below the coastguard cottages returning to the top again just west of the coastguard cottages. From here it continues first by path and then on the grass verge down to Hele Bay, where there is a café should you need refreshment. Turn off the Combe Martin road into Beach Road past the Hele Bay car park and the Path begins opposite the children's paddling pool. The Path climbs over and around Hillsborough (137 metres) providing a splendid bird's-eye view of Ilfracombe, looking down on Blythe's Cave, Broadstrand Beach and across to the tiny Chapel of St. Nicholas on Lantern Hill – a landmark for seamen since the Reformation when it was first used as a lighthouse. The Path takes you above Rapparee Cove, passing Larkstone Beach on the right and the harbour, to come out in Broad Street.

On arriving in Broad Street you may wish to use the rest

Ilfracombe

of the day to tour Ilfracombe, visiting Lantern Hill, Capstone Hill, the Quay and Lifeboat House. There are many cafés, restaurants and hotels providing every kind of food and beverage. Or, if you are in Ilfracombe on one of the three days when the White Funnel Steamer calls, why not use this opportunity to visit Lundy? It is possible to walk the whole of the Lundy coastline before the steamer returns in the afternoon.

It would be unfair to allow you to leave Ilfracombe without telling you the story of the Red Petticoats. On 22 February 1797, four French ships were sighted off Ilfracombe, where the French commander sank several English coasting vessels by forcing them to scuttle. At that time most of Ilfracombe's 200 full-time sailors were away serving with the Royal Navy. The women of the town, realising the danger of possible invasion, removed their traditional red petticoats and draped them around their shoulders like scarlet cloaks, then took up prominent positions on the high ground around the town.

The sight of the red petticoats convinced the French that Ilfracombe was garrisoned with a strong military force and they hurriedly sailed away.

Leave Broad Street along St. James Place and follow it into Wilder Road. Turn right along Bath Place through the tunnel opposite into Granville Road, and turn left into Torr Walk Avenue which leads up to Torr Walk through a wooden gate past a sign reading *Public Footpath to Lee Bay*. Farther on over a stile is a National Trust sign reading *Flat Point*. This is now a gentle walk after what has gone before.

49

Along the old coast road, from here to Westward Ho!, the coastline is designated part of the North Devon Area of Outstanding Natural Beauty and, as the signposts indicate, a considerable amount of it comes under the protection of the National Trust. The Flat Point area ends its western limit at a gate leading down a narrow, hedged and banked country lane towards Lee Bay, passing on the right the Blue Mushroom Tearoom. Half-way down the hill on the left is a path across fields, through a gate passing a signpost indicating the pretty thatched cottaged village of Lee, with its old pub, *The Grampus*, nestled in Fuchsia Valley, so-called because of the abundance of fuchsias which, with rhododendrons, make a colourful spectacle.

The Path continues down the lane running out alongside the Lee Bay Hotel. It continues past Chapel Cottage Restaurant, with its charming flower garden almost at the sea edge, around the seaweed-covered rocks of the beach – surrounded like Porlock Weir by sheer cliffs – to climb again to the tarmac road to Morte Point. After 360 metres, on the right, is a gate bearing a National Trust sign reading *Damage Cliffs*. To the right of the gate a second sign says *Footpath to Bull Point* and the Path climbs to the open tops of Damage Hue looking over Pensport Rock to Bull Point, over two spring-fed combes enclosing (at 90 metres) three standing stones. Then across the track to Bull Point lighthouse which is open to visitors from 2 p.m. The Path then drops down to Rockham Bay where it narrows and becomes uneven and boulder-strewn.

Walking along the ebbing tide at Rockham Bay I sensed, rather than heard, the regular thump of a ship's engine for some time before the White Funnel steamer to Lundy hove into view around the point, followed by the scarlet-painted, converted ice-breaker *Polar Bear* – the island's own vessel. They slowly disappeared ahead of me into the heat haze hiding Lundy from sight. Around Morte Point the turbulent waters of its tidal race emphasize the menacing quality of these fractured reefs tapering away into the sea, illustrating perfectly how the geological structure has changed yet again. Now the cliffs cut across the rock groups, the Middle Devonian smooth and glossy, the grey and purple slates of the Morte Beds resting firmly on the Ilfracombe Beds, showing a great diversity of form and creating the most exciting rock scenery.

The dreaded Morte Stone off the Point – a dangerous sunken reef of rocks to westward which gave its name to the nearby village, was christened 'Death Stone' by the Normans, and many ill-fated ships and crews have been lost rounding Morte Point. In the winter of 1852 five ships went down here, and it is not surprising that the lighthouse was finally erected at Bull Point in 1879, with its very loud fog-horn to warn off ships in foggy weather. There is a

Toward
Morte Poin
from
Woolacomb

legend attached to this stone, insisting that any man who is master of his wife possesses the power to remove the stone; but, to the time of writing, no man has done so!

Rounding Morte Point we change direction, walking almost north-south rather than east-west, past Grunta Beach where you can join the road off to Morthoe village and see the fine Norman church of St. Mary Magdalene, believed to contain the burial tomb of William de Tracey, one of the murderers of Thomas à Becket.

After Combes Gate the Path passes the famous shell beach of Barricane – where many varieties of delicately coloured tropical shells are washed ashore by Atlantic currents from the Caribbean – and finally down to the sands at Woolacombe.

Woolacombe has grown very quickly out of a cluster of scattered farms into a holiday resort, climbing ever higher up the slopes towards Morte Point, and seemingly determined to become the Newquay of North Devon. Like that resort it owes its popularity to the vast expanse of sand covering the five kilometres of Morte Bay between Morte and Baggy Points, protected by the dunes of Woolacombe Warren and providing the ideal holiday beach.

The Path enters Woolacombe alongside Barricane Beach, joining The Esplanade to turn right and make its unmarked way through the centre of the resort. It passes the end of Beach Road, then Barton Road, picking up a Coast Path sign pointing to the dunes of Woolacombe Warren running parallel with Chalacombe Road. It stays on the Warren all the way to the end of Morte Bay, running out between Putsborough and Napps Cliff. But it is hard going – an undulating surface of soft drifting sand and marram grass – and my advice is to take to the beach. Here the sand is firm and flat. On a warm sunlit day with a cool breeze off the sea it makes ideal walking conditions, but, of course, can only be negotiated at low tide.

The Path leaves the beach at Vention, by a house on the beach with a large relief of Neptune on its wall, and goes up stone steps, past a car park and a National Trust sign to Baggy Point, alongside an acorn Coast Path marker. You go over Napps Cliff, climbing a stile with an acorn signpost, before moving around the verges of cabbage, turnip and wheat straw fields. There are wonderful cliff-top views across Wheeler's Stone in the bay, and back across the Coast Path from Minehead. This area is a paradise for ornithologists; the south-westerly gales of the autumn 'wreck' many birds on these cliffs and kittiwakes, auks, gannets and shearwaters are frequently seen between September and November. Migrating finches, larks and a great number of chaffinches and pipits can be viewed from the headlands, as well as colonies of herring gulls, shags, cormorants, fulmars, occasional ravens, and stock doves nesting on the cliff edges.

Gannets and shearwaters

The Path, after passing the unmanned coastguard look-out turns back to run north-south again before dropping down towards Croyde – but not entering the village. At Croyde Bay, after passing the National Trust car park on the left, the Coast Path turns right on to the beach around the wall of the hotel. Crossing Croyde Sands to the westward side under Croyde Burrows, it climbs stone steps and follows around the cliff edge, skirting ploughed fields – planted, on this occasion, with cauliflowers and turnips. Finally it runs up a narrow alley formed by the wall of Chesit Cliff Hotel on the right and a weird wooden construction on the left, to come out on the tarmac road between Croyde and Braunton. Turn right across this road and a few metres down on the left another signpost marks the Path as running just above and parallel with the road. It runs through bracken, gorse and brambles all the way until, opposite the Saunton Sands Hotel, it ends at a gate alongside the road (B3231) which has to be crossed to pick up the Path across Braunton Burrows.

Saunton Sands
to Westward Ho!

6½ kilometres   Map 6

At the time of writing, there is only one short section of Coast Path between the Saunton Sands Hotel and Westward Ho! which runs behind Braunton Burrows for a time before doubling back and turning at right-angles across Braunton Great Field to Braunton village.

The route starts across the B3231 from the gate. It passes around the front of the hotel to the right, on to the dunes close by a beach café before joining a signposted narrow pathway of thick brambles, gorse and thistles around the extreme edge of the golf course and coming out at the side of the club house on the B3231 again. About 270 metres to the right is a tiny lane with a Coast Path marker indicating right for 30 metres to a wooden gate with an acorn symbol. This leads to a second gate across a field and joins the golf course once more following acorn-marked public bridleway signs. From now on follow absolutely the direction of these signposts; if in doubt, hug the extreme edge of the links – bordered by a bramble hedge – through a succession of alder groves until finally passing through a gate in front of two large signs *Braunton Burrows Nature Reserve* and in *red*, DANGER – *Ministry of Defence Ranges*. Do not pass when red flag is flying. Continue past these signs (looking for the red flag, of course) until reaching a Nature Conservancy blue marker with a white arrow indicating the bridleway, turning sharp left to come out in a car park leading on to what is known as the American Road At present the Coast Path turns left on this road until reaching Sandy Lane and a farm with buildings both sides of the road. Turn right here and stay on the road to Second Field Lane where the Path ends in Braunton.

The present walk is only temporary and you may prefer to take the route which the Coast Path will finally follow, along a local path out to the Groynes around Crow Point, to enter the Burrows by the Broadwalk.

Braunton Burrows consists of 1,000 hectares of dune system owned by the Christie Estate Trust, Devon. The Ministry of Defence lease 600 hectares, which is in turn leased from them by the Nature Conservancy Council for

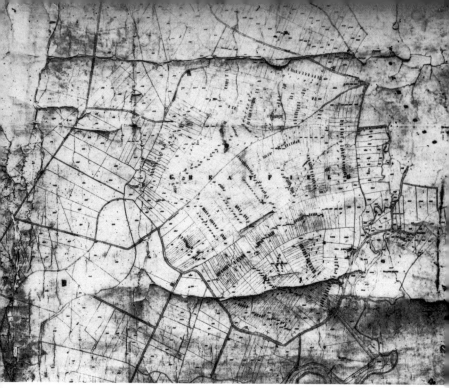

Ancient map of Braunton Great Field

the management of wildlife conservation. Military training still takes place in this area, however, and at such times red flags are flown, sentries posted and the area is closed to visitors.

The reserve is open to walkers and horse-riders along public paths. Visitors are asked to stay on these routes, as indiscriminate trampling through the dunes causes great damage to the thin carpet of vegetation holding together the sand and gravel. Wind greatly affects this vegetation, blowing the sand away, creating gullies and areas of mobile sand, and in order to encourage dune formation and lessen this wind erosion, fences of wooden palings have been set across gullies to trap the sand. Extensive inland areas of the Burrows have been planted with marram grass, to help stabilize the dunes, as happens naturally where sand couch grass and sand sedge grow, closer to the sea.

Farther back from the beach wind-scour has created large wet areas of fresh water known as 'slacks', or referred to locally as 'pans'. This is an ideal habitat for bog vegetation such as creeping willow, and beneath grows an abundance of sea pearlwort and marsh helleborine, an unusual orchid with purplish brown and white flowers. Also the extremely rare fen orchid and the mosses

Dicranella varia, Drepanocladis aduncus and *D. sendtneri*,
together with the tender pale green liverwort forming a
patchwork against the sand. The blown shell and rock sand
from the beach – high in calcium carbonate – is ideal for
hundreds of species of plants, some not found anywhere
else in Great Britain, for example, water germander,
round-headed club rush and French toadflax.

Insect life is also plentiful, particularly during the
summer months when red admiral, painted lady, small
copper, common blue, small tortoiseshell, peacock and
fritillary butterflies are seen along with day-flying cin-
nabar and spot burnet moths; whilst the ruddy sympetrum
and golden-ringed dragonfly are common after the month
of June. In the warm evenings smoky or common wainscot
moths appear. The area is rich in the *Orthoptera* family of
insects, including the common field grasshopper, common
ground hopper, meadow grasshopper, mottled grasshopper
and the great green bush cricket.

Fox holes and trails indicate the size of the fox population. Rabbits, once decimated by myxomatosis, seem to
be on the increase and where the scattered sandhills merge
into sandy pasture and shrubs grow there are field mice,
shrews and voles. The sand also attracts lizards and its
calcium carbonate provides the necessary diet for many
snails.

Like Morte Point, Braunton Burrows provides a resting
place for migrant birds – the most rare being short-eared
owls. Merlin, harrier, wheatear and shellduck breed on
the dunes.

The warm air of the dunes during August and September
is impregnated with the scent of evening primroses whose
yellow flowers open in the evening to be pollinated by
night-flying moths.

It is not essential to follow the Coast Path back to
Sandy Lane Farm. Instead take the footpath on the
embankment around Horsey Island to Velator Bridge to
meet the old Barnstaple to Braunton railway line. Closed
some time ago, the track bed will soon find a new use as a
public footpath and this will provide an ideal path along
the Taw estuary into Barnstaple. Another route off the
dunes is along the tarmac road to Gallowell. Here, on the
left, is a centuries-old public footpath cutting diagonally
across Braunton Great Field to come out in Second Field
Lane, Braunton.

Braunton Great Field is part of a way of life left over
from the sixteenth century, and is one of the only three
surviving open-field systems left in England. These large
areas of arable land were divided into narrow strips for
cultivation, separated by dykes, furrows or unploughed
narrow sections of land known locally as 'balk'. In Braunton Parish Council office there is a large map showing the
division of this field some centuries ago when it was

Short-eared owl

farmed by well over 100 families. Today these are down to a tiny handful.

From Braunton the bus from Ilfracombe will take you all the way to Westward Ho! without changing – through Barnstaple, Fremington, Yelland, Instow, Bideford and Appledore. However, for those of you not wishing to travel all that distance by bus, here are some alternatives.

Stay on the bus to Instow and alight at Instow Quay. Here the rivers Taw and Torridge meet, creating a magnificent estuary and containing some of the loneliest spots in all Devon. From the quay a ferry crosses to Appledore during the summer months – the running times are written on a board. Should you feel like a walk along the river Taw before crossing, walk back a short distance towards Yelland until reaching Lane End. Pick up a right-of-way across Instow Sands and continue around Instow Barton Marsh opposite Crow Point on Braunton Burrows. Cross a weir before Yelland Power Station, passing between the power station and the jetty with colliers continuously unloading, and on to East Yelland Marsh. Here, some years ago, I spent an entertaining day endeavouring to catch flat fish using what looked like a straightened-out garden rake fitted with barbs; 'pranging' it was called by the locals teaching me. A few of them earned a precarious living in this manner; also by picking mussels and the most succulent cockles from nearby. But I doubt if any of them survive in this fashion today. Return to the quay along the same path and leave for Appledore on the ferry.

Another interesting and pleasant walk can be enjoyed by staying on the bus from Braunton until it crosses the bridge and turns right on to the quay in Bideford. Alight here to cross the road and walk along the quay, with the

Round-headed
club rush

Golden-ringed
dragonfly

Marsh helleborine

Water germander

Wheatear

Common blue

Small copper

Fen orchid

Peacock

French (sand)
toadflax

Six-spot burnet
moth

Creeping willow

Ruddy-sympetrum
dragonfly

Sea pearlwort

Great green bush
cricket

river on your right and in the direction of Appledore. You will pass a statue of Charles Kingsley alongside Victoria Park, Bideford football ground, a cattle market on the left, a bus depot and Bideford shipyard (sadly closed) on the right. After passing the shipyard take the route to the left along Chircombe Lane for a short distance, then turn sharp right in Limens Lane bringing you back to the river again. It is possible to continue along the 'river bank walk' to the right, but it travels along the river's edge through thick black mud that oozes up over boot level. From now on it is a fine walk to Cleave Houses and on to The Cleave.

Continue on through wooded river slopes, bordered by National Trust land, until the path finally ends by the covered Appledore shipbuilders' yard at Bidna. An alternative way, after leaving the National Trust land, is to take the path to the left leading to Hyde Barton, passing that house to come out on Churchill Way at Bloody Corner in Northam. A Victorian local historian called Chappell believed this to be the site of the famous battle in which Hubba, the Dane, was defeated (but see page 31). So he erected a stone bearing this inscription:

> Stop! Stranger stop!
> Near this spot
> Lies buried
> King Hubba, the Dane
> Who was slain by King Alfred the Great
> In a bloody retreat.

Follow Churchill Way to the right, branching off right down Pitt Hill to the quay, leading into Churchfield Road and then Irsha Street. Here the routes from the Instow/Appledore ferry and the path from Appledore Shipbuilders at Bidna all meet.

Appledore harbour at low tide

Irsha Street is long and narrow running parallel with the waterfront to High Cliff Terrace, past alleyways, courtyards and tiny slipways leading down to the rocky, tidal foreshore. It was used by a number of small boat builders throughout the centuries, but alas no more. Some of the cottages date back to the seventeenth century but most are mid-nineteenth century, and a great many are holiday homes – used in the summer and left empty throughout the long months of winter. Continue along Irsha Street past the Custom House; serving all ports on the Taw and Torridge, it has been situated here since 1671 collecting dues on cargo ships using these waters. Carry on past the lifeboat station, using a field to the left running past Hinks' Boatyard.

Leave the boatyard walking along the road away from Irsha Street and take the first turn right bringing you to the Northam Burrows Country Park which has its own signposts. Keep close to the coast; at low tide you can safely walk the beach; if not you will have to negotiate the Pebble Ridge.

The Pebble Ridge is about three kilometres long, 15 metres wide and 6 metres high. It protects from the sea not only Northam Burrows but the Royal North Devon Golf Club, formed in 1863 and one of the oldest links in Great Britain. Often during periods of high tides and fierce gales the ridge is breached and sometimes flattened, and a great deal of it has been enclosed in wire mesh to try and hold the pebbles in position.

For many centuries repairing breaches in the ridge has been the responsibility of the 'Potwallopers' of Northam, who undertook the task in exchange for certain rights dating back to feudal times. These rights were made available to all who 'boiled their pots on their own hearths' within the Northam area (hence their name), and allowed them to graze their stock on the Burrows; also to use the port of Appledore as a 'free' harbour. The Potwallopers defended their rights vigorously, even going to court in 1716 and winning a case, known as the 'Northam award'. If the ridge did not exist the whole area inside it would become an enormous salt marsh, and so every August the Potwallopers assemble on the ridge and work throughout the day restoring and repairing it, refreshed by having food and cider brought to them.

Follow the track along the top of Pebble Ridge all the way into Westward Ho! and rejoin the Coast Path immediately beyond the slipway leading to the promenade and passing the Elizabethan Club.

Westward Ho! to Clovelly

19 kilometres Maps 7 – 8

Westward Ho! is unique in being the only holiday resort to grow from the publication of a novel – Charles Kingsley's *Westward Ho!*, published in 1855. The foundation stone for the first building was laid in 1863. Kingsley, when he later visited the resort, disliked what he saw. Were he able to view today's sprawl of caravan sites and holiday chalets, I imagine he would care for it even less.

In a row of 12 large Victorian houses, known as Kipling Terrace, and now mostly derelict, tucked away from the public eye behind an iron gate, is a plaque of grey, veined Welsh stone with these words: *This terrace of 12 houses was occupied by the United Services College, September 1874 to March 1904. Rudyard Kipling was educated here January 1878 to July 1882 under Cornell Price, Esq, MA, BCL, first headmaster.*

Here Kipling stored away the memories that were later to become his famous school story *Stalky & Co.* In his memoirs *Something of myself for my friends – known and unknown* Kipling has described his days at Westward Ho!

The Coast Path starts again almost under Kipling Terrace, across a flat area of grassland used as a playing field by those who do not care for the beach.

The first section of the Path is flat and level for a very good reason; it follows the route of the old Westward Ho! to Bideford railway line, opened in 1908 but closed in 1917. It passes through the remains of embankments and cuttings all the way to Cornborough where the line branched inland, and the Path starts dropping down to the beach at Abbotsham.

This walk, before the Path begins to plunge and climb once again, is extremely pleasant with the tors rising away to the left and the sea beneath. It is described in *Stalky & Co.*

'They were walking through a combe half full of old, high furze in gay bloom that ran up to a fringe of brambles and dense wood of mixed timber and hollies. It was as though one half of the combe were filled with golden fire to the cliffs edge. The tough stems parted before them and it was a window opened on a far view

roded coast near
aunton Down

63

of Lundy, and the deep sea sluggishly nosing the pebbles a couple of hundred feet below. They could hear young jackdaws squawking on the ledges, the hiss and jabber of a nest of hawks somewhere out of sight; great grey and black gulls screamed against the jackdaws, the heavy scented acres of bloom were alive with low-nesting birds, singing or silent as the shadow of the wheeling hawks passed and returned, and on the naked turf across the combe rabbits thumped and frolicked.'

And so it remains today, unchanged except for the new stiles with acorn signs and blue and yellow arrows and triangles marking the way, and wire separating walkers from farm fields. The Path goes past Cornborough with two lime-kilns on the beach once fired by anthracite from a seam on the face of Green Cliff during 1805. Then on to Abbotsham, so named because it was an endowment of Tavistock Abbey whose lands and properties once stretched from Dorset to the Isles of Scilly. Here is access to another pebbled beach. Between Abbotsham and Greencliff, looking seaward, is tiny Greencliff Rock and inland a small hill made famous in 1922 by a racecourse running around it, with the surrounding hills providing superb grandstands. The Path continues over Westacott Cliff and the Rowden along a track cut through thick undergrowth, steeply climbing and descending, sometimes using man-made steps hammered into the crumbling path. Then it crosses a stream, climbs over a stile bearing a signpost indicating the Coast Path in both directions and passes the path running down from the Portledge Hotel – for 800 years the home of the Coffin family – to a delightful secluded beach with some sand between the boulders, and a once white beach hut.

Crossing the weir by a footbridge to pick up the old coastguard track, the walker should stay with this track all the way to Peppercombe. Here the wooded slopes of the valley of the Pippa may be carpeted with bluebells, foxgloves, campions, primroses, or many species of ferns, and alive with the continuous sounds of songbirds and of water moving over its boulder-strewn bed, before dropping steeply and sharply to the sea. The surrounding rocks are warm in contrasting shades of red balanced by yellows and browns, coloured by the presence here (and nowhere else along this northern coastline) of Triassic marls.

Leave Peppercombe over a footbridge by the Path, signposted and yellow-arrowed. This curves back around the combe, climbs more steps driven into the track with wooden stakes, and passes a field containing the site of the ancient earthworks of Peppercombe Castle. It makes a hard but not too steep climb through Sloo Woods, over two stiles and, on leaving Worthygate Wood, a third stile at right-angles to the path with an acorn signpost indicating

Great spotted
woodpecker

Redstart

Red campion

Wood anemone

Nuthatch

Primrose

a farm track. This continues until the climb down to Buck's Mills, passing above on the right another ancient earthwork, and lower down on the left a coastguard look-out with the coastguard's name *Braund* prominently and proudly displayed (with good reason as we shall see). This brings the walker to Buck's Mills.

Buck's Mills is a charming rugged cove enclosed by densely wooded cliffs, ending with a steep inclined plane built to carry away lime brought across from Pembroke-shire and used locally to neutralize the acid in the fields after burning in Buck's Mills' two lime-kilns. One of these is a splendid construction with a circular 'keep' and buttress often mistaken by visitors for a ruined castle.

Today the cottages belong almost entirely to second-home owners or are let to summer visitors, and only a handful of local people live here all the year round. At one time every cottage was lived in by a member of the Braund family.

> 'The Braunds of Buksh
> They swim like ducks
> A mighty race are they . . . .'

Who were the Braunds of Buksh? While it is true that the village of Buck's Mills was, for over 200 years, their kingdom, and the head of the family – who lived in the last cottage standing high above the beach – was always called the King of Buksh, very little is known of their ancestry. John Lloyd Warden Page in his book *The Coast of Devon* described them as being 'unlike any folk in adjoining villages both in speech, manner and complexion', and certainly their dark, shining hair, swarthy good looks, brown eyes and different style of speech marked them as a race apart from other Devonians. One suggestion is that they came from seven survivors of a Spanish galleon sunk at the time of the Armada, who settled in the village and married local girls; but a recent theory describes them as descendants of a once powerful tribe at the time of Carac-tacus known as the Carnabii, who sailed to Great Britain in a tiny craft from Spain 3,000 years ago. The Braunds were superlative seamen and fishermen snatching a living off this grim shore. Having no harbour they virtually launched their sturdy little boats off the cliff face, running over razor-edged rocks to reach deep water. Local legends say the Braunds went to sea in weather so foul no vessel dare put out over Bideford bar, and a score of ships would be sheltering in the lee of Lundy. Before the day of the Clovelly lifeboat the Braund menfolk, with their wives watching from the cliffs, would launch their boats on errands of mercy rescuing mariners. One of their fishing boats can still be seen in the fascinating Maritime Museum on the quay in Exeter.

The Path continues behind the tea shop, between two cottages, rising up through woods with a signpost at the top; through a gate between two buildings, then crosses a field with a fine view out to sea before entering the grounds of Walland Cary. This estate takes its name from Henry de la Wallen, lord of these lands during the reign of Edward I (1272–1307). Walland Cary today is a chalet village complete with swimming pool and country club. The Path runs along a well-signposted route through the middle of it, to come out at the camp rubbish dump resplendent with all the tin and plastic debris of contemporary living.

Leaving the holiday village the Coast Path skirts a field alongside an electrified fence, and here it is essential to stay on the verge for in the field corner it re-enters a wood to the right. Unfortunately this is by an unsightly motor car dump. Leave the wood over a stile, go down a dip, still skirting a field by the wood, to pass through large iron gates along a well-worn path crossing a field and running down a hollow. A stile and a signpost indicate steps through a wood, across a small stream leading up gravel-covered steps to a right turn on Hobby Drive.

Hobby Drive twists and turns its way along the cliff edge through five kilometres of luxuriant woods dropping down to the sea from here to Clovelly. It was built in the early nineteenth century and was constructed as a hobby by the man who then owned the whole of Clovelly – Sir James Hamlyn Williams. There are two conflicting theories concerning the manner in which it was built. One insists

Lundy steamer and puffins

it was undertaken by Napoleonic prisoners-of-war, the other that it was a deliberate attempt by Sir James to provide employment for the men of Clovelly during a depressed period in its history.

The Coast Path threads its way down through steeply wooded slopes of sycamore, oak, beech, rowan and the occasional holly, passing seats on the path edge positioned to provide superb views down on to rows of neat, freshly-painted cottages with flower-filled gardens tumbling down cobblestoned streets to Quay Pool and the fourteenth-century pier. There the waters of high tide reflect back the luminescent orange of the lifeboat riding the swell on permanent station; it leaves only to run from the weather and shelter behind the northern cliffs of Lundy Island.

Clovelly's prosperity dates back to the Carys of Clovelly Court who inherited it from the Giffard family in 1370. They remained Lords of the Manor for 400 years during which time they built the stone pier that made Clovelly a safe harbour for the fishing boats seeking shoals of herring along this coast, and established a local fleet of 70 vessels. In 1730 the estate was sold to the squire of Woolfardis-worthy, Zachary Hamlyn, and a descendant of that family retains possession today.

Charles Kingsley came here as a young boy, his father leaving Holne on Dartmoor to become curate and later rector of the parish. Charles immortalized Clovelly in *Westward Ho!*, and included Will Cary among his charac-ters. The original William Cary presented the fine, black-oak pulpit to All Saints Church in 1634. Clovelly also gained publicity and popularity from the publication of Charles Dickens' *A Message from the Sea*. Adverse publi-city, however, came from the *Legend of the Clovelly cannibals*. This pamphlet, printed in 1740 and once housed in Bideford Public Library, tells of a family called Gregg. John Gregg the father, his wife, eight sons, six daughters, 18 grandsons and 14 granddaughters – all cannibals. They made a speciality of carrying off innocent travellers including children, of robbing then murdering them and finally dragging their bodies into a cave beneath the cliffs to be eaten. This legend is repeated on Dartmoor with the notorious Gubbins family of Lydford Gorge whose leader – known as the King – died on the sword of Salvation Yeo in the pages of *Westward Ho!*.

Before continuing along the Coast Path you may wish to spend some time in Clovelly. Should you arrive at the height of the holiday season, it would be advisable to look around the village early in the morning, or after the crowds have left in the evening.

Red kite   Buzzard   Montagu's harrier   Peregrine falcon

Hobby

Kestrel

Buzzard

Clovelly
to Hartland Quay
17 kilometres

The route out of Clovelly leads down from the gate of
Hobby Drive above Mount Pleasant – an area given as a
war memorial to the National Trust by Christina Hamlyn.
On the left is a large gate signed to *Angels Wings, Gallantry Bower and Mouth Mill*. Go through the gate,
crossing the park where a signpost indicates the cliff path
following alongside a fence; pass a wooden kissing gate
and continue until reaching another such gate in iron.
Enter and keep to the right along a path leading to a
stone-built shelter with marvellous views back towards
Minehead. The Path then passes close to the cliff edge
until reaching a clearing in the wood where stands *Angels
Wings*. This is an extraordinary wooden garden seat with
a cedar shingled canopy supported and surrounded by
ornately carved wings; some in pairs, issuing from either
side of an angel's head, others on their own. It carries a

Angels Wings

ackchurch
ck

71

Storm brewing over Hartland Point

sign *Built in 1826, restored by a few devoted friends 1934, in memory of Marion Stucky who loved Clovelly.* It also carries a great many examples of modern vandalism.

Rest here to absorb the view before moving on along the cliff path. An alternative path is arrowed through the woods but it does not enjoy the breath-taking scenery of the cliff route leading to Gallantry Bower. A high, wind-swept headland with a sheer drop of 120 metres to the sea below, its name derives either from the actions of lovers forbidden to marry and leaping from here to their doom, or from being the site of the village gallows.

After the Path has once again converged with a number of others (all providing delightful alternative walks), you will find, through a gap in the rocks on the right, a flat platform where a seat has been placed with a magnificent panoramic sea view – in perfect peace and solitude. It is known locally as *Miss Wodall's seat* after a Mouth Mill lady who had the seat placed in what she considered to be the most enchanting spot in the world.

Returning to the Path, start descending to where Mouth Mill and Windbury Head can be seen below. Follow a zig-zag path, passing the summer house built by Dame Diana Hamlyn in 1820, and restored by friends of Christina Hamlyn for her eightieth birthday in 1935, and on into Mouth Mill.

Mouth Mill offers another chance to take off your boots and soak your feet in the sea. It has a beach typical of those we have passed since leaving Appledore, mostly pebbles and rocks with an area of reasonably flat grassland behind, framed by woods on both slopes of the valley. To the right of the beach is Blackchurch Rock with its sea-worn hole in the shape of a Gothic arch; left are the splendours of Windbury waterfall. Once it was possible to obtain refreshment at Mouth Mill in one of the two cottages close to the ruined lime-kiln; not today, alas. Leave by crossing the stream, climbing steeply through woods, over an acorn-posted stile and skirting a field edge where pheasant called as I journeyed. More wooden steps and a stile lead around a field edge with uninterrupted Channel views. Negotiate four more stiles before dropping steeply down into woods again; cross a wooden footbridge with a handrail and climb again past two signposts – one indicating a circular woodland walk to the cliffs (a most rewarding detour), the other the Coast Path climbing out of the woods at Windbury Point with a last chance to look back and down to Blackchurch Rock.

The Path continues through National Trust lands along Brownsham Cliff. This descends towards Brownsham Farm often using log steps, across another wooden bridge spanning a stream which tumbles down the combe, and climbs more steps to a stile leading into a field. Follow the field edge off to the right indicated by a yellow arrowed signpost, over a stile skirting a ploughed field, and continue along a well-signed easy route to Eldern Point.

Guillemots, razorbill, cormorants; fulmars and shag in flight

Dipper

Eldern Point provides another glorious lookout position
for views across to Lundy and the Welsh coast, particularly if you leave the Path and walk out to its exposed
safe limits. The Path continues through a gate with a
signpost and, farther along, passes a very steep descent to
Shipload Bay – the only genuine stretch of sandy beach
between Westward Ho! and the Cornish border. This is a
favourite bathing retreat for local families who park their
cars at East Titchberry Farm and walk the rest of the way.
From Shipload Bay the first attempts to lay a cable under
the sea to Lundy were made, but the powerful tides and
Atlantic rollers proved too strong and it was swept away.

The Coast Path leaving here passes between the peri-
meter fence of the radar station and the sea, turning at
right-angles towards Barley Bay – another magnificent
view-point but spoilt, in my opinion, by an unsightly car
park. It turns left again around the old emergency water
catchment area before the gates leading to the lighthouse.
Hartland Point lighthouse was built in 1874 and Bishop
Temple of Exeter (later Archbishop of Canterbury)
officiated at the blessing; it can be visited on weekdays
after 2 p.m.

The Path, leaving by a gate, continues straight ahead
to join a field behind the coastguard lookout on Blagdon

74

Cliffs, and on to the Upright Cliff.

The Coast Path has changed direction yet again, turning at right-angles southwards and hugging the cliff edge. The appearance and geology of the landscape has also changed. The hog's back cliffs which have formed the coastline from Minehead have ended, being replaced by a series of near vertical escarpments with flat, grass-covered tops. These geological formations were created by the enormous pressure exerted by the actions of the sea on these predominantly west-facing cliffs. This followed after a lateral pressure, over 300 million years ago, which pushed up the neat horizontal layers of Devonian and carboniferous sediments, wriggling and contorting them, fashioning wedged-shaped synclines and mushroom-shaped anticlines, thus causing vertical tiltings in these cliffs stretching from Hartland westward. From here to Bude is undoubtedly some of the most exciting rock scenery in the whole country, with the cliffs cutting across the rock groups in a series of parallel ridges, often folded one over the other with deep grooves separating them. The harder rock has formed headlands rising at right-angles to the coastline; whilst softer rock beds contain caverns. Farther inland deep valleys have been carved by swift-running streams which, at the cliff edges, tumble as dazzling waterfalls.

From Upright Cliff the route to Hartland Quay can be clearly seen with the Tower on the Warren acting as a beacon which we shall eventually pass straight ahead; on the right are the northern cliffs of Smoothlands Valley. The Coast Path drops down to a stream known as Titch-

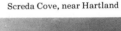

Screda Cove, near Hartland

berry Water with a route leading to the beach. Across the stream are a series of rapids before the Coast Path heads inland, up the valley and over an elaborate stone bridge with a wooden handrail. A steep climb up the other side leads into a field and heads back towards the sea into Smoothlands Valley. This used to be the natural bed of the Titchberry Water until the sea captured areas of Smoothlands Valley, separating it and forcing the original stream to find an alternative sea outlet farther to the north. It is a bewitching place, quite unlike any area walked through on this route. It invites the traveller to rest and enjoy its peace and beauty before moving on down the valley to Damehole Point where the Path goes out to the extremities of the Point. This affords dramatic views to Lundy.

After bearing close to a small waterfall behind Damehole Point the Path continues up Blegberry Cliff. In the distance, commanding the landscape for miles around, can be seen the Late Perpendicular tower of Stoke Church of St. Nectan, the highest in Devon – only to lose sight of it again as the Path drops down to cross an old stone bridge over Blegberry Water. Here is a far more exciting waterfall, the water from which seems to disappear mysteriously as its fall reaches the beach. This is a favourite spot of the local population who leave their cars at the old fortified farmhouse of Blegberry, dating back to 1627.

Now the Path climbs steeply before dropping sharply down to Blackpool Mill in the valley and leading up to Hartland Abbey. This was founded as a college for secular canons during the eleventh century and converted by Geoffrey de Dinant into an Augustinian abbey in 1189. Today it is a private dwelling owing much of its architecture to rebuilding around 1860. It has given its name to the stream, known locally as the Abbey River, with pools and miniature waterfalls where the old mill house stands on its banks. The Path, passing around and behind to the left of this building, goes through a kissing gate, over a stone bridge to climb very steeply again towards Dyer's Lookout, which provides a superb opportunity to gaze back over the route you have travelled, before moving on towards the Warren Tower – an easy walk from now on.

Very little is known about the Tower although this has not stopped a great deal being written concerning it. Most accounts suggest that it had no real purpose other than perhaps as a lookout – some say for Barbary pirates. All seem to agree it was finally converted into a summer house by the owners of Hartland Abbey. Passing the Tower, the Path goes on to the Old Rocket Apparatus House used at one time, as its name suggests, to house life-saving gear. The Path continues over a stile and off to the left, avoiding Hartland Quay, following the old fishermen's track on the northern side of the quay leading to the hotel.

Hartland Quay was once an extremely busy port for Hartland. The building of the quay was authorized by Act of Parliament in 1566, and sponsored by Sir W. Courtenay, Sir Walter Raleigh, Sir Francis Drake and Sir John Hawkins. Around the quay were built cottages for coastguards, and a thriving working community of fishermen, farm labourers and workers in the three lime-kilns. There was also a malt house that provided ale for the inn, known over the years as The Hooper, The New Inn, and The Mariners' Rest, and it must be the only hostelry in the country ordered to close (during 1874) for excessive drinking. It also contained a bank authorized to issue £1 and £5 notes to facilitate the importing of coal, lime, timber, building materials, fertilizer (including guano), glass, and during 1616 lead for repairing St. Nectan's Church. It exported corn and malt.

The harbour remained until the last century when severe gales during 1887, and again in the winter of 1896, completely washed it away. However, in September 1979 I witnessed the re-opening of a new quay. It had been built over a period of two years entirely by the labour and at the expense of the people of Hartland, and the small boats went to sea to fish and put down crab pots for the first time since 1925. (For Hartland, see page 106.)

Terns circling over crab boat

Hartland Quay
to Marsland Mouth

8½ kilometres   Maps 9 – 10

This final section of the walk from Hartland Quay to Marsland Mouth includes some of the finest coastal scenery in Great Britain but, although it is a short journey, it can at times be hard going, adding further substance to the nickname it has earned for itself of 'The Iron Coast'.

The Path leaves the Quay through a section of the Devon Naturalist Trust Nature Reserve, passing Screda Point and heading for St. Catherine's Tor. It skirts another valley captured by the sea, once the course of the stream known as Margery Water which used to run out into the sea at Hartland Quay, but which now cascades to the beach as a waterfall, behind St. Catherine's Tor.

St. Catherine's Tor stands exposed like one half of a giant slab cake sliced through with a sharp knife. The Path follows Margery Water, over short springy grass that is good to walk on and which fills the air with the scent of wild thyme. It is believed a chapel once stood on the summit of the Tor, built in the fourteenth century and dedicated to St. Catherine. No evidence of this remains but occasional debris found on the beach after the ravages of coastal erosion seems to suggest some kind of religious building once existed here. The path to the beach has also disappeared as a result of this erosion so it is necessary to move on inland, climbing the steep cliff south of the Tor to look down upon the most exciting waterfall yet encountered – at Speke's Mill Mouth.

Linger at Speke's Mill Mouth, and enjoy to the full the spectacle of this twin fall of water dropping 16 metres to the beach below; an experience you will always remember. If you are fit, well shod and prepared to take a risk, you could climb down to the beach and move away to your left under the cliff, before starting to climb back up the rocks that form the right bank of the stream. This will take you through a series of small falls eventually leading to the main drop – a breath-taking sight and a just reward for all your efforts. Of course, if there has been a period of heavy rain, or during the winter months, such a feat is out of the question.

Green Ranger aground 1962

The Path continues up the valley crossing a wooden bridge, to turn right leaving Stansford Hill back to the cliff edge again. At Longpeak you will pass the rusting remains of winch gear, hawsers and metal left behind from the salvage of the *Green Ranger* – a Royal Fleet Auxiliary tanker under tow, which broke its cable and was wrecked on the rocks of Longpeak in November 1962. The seven men aboard were rescued by breeches-buoy after feats of great hardship and bravery had been endured by all the rescue units involved, including coastguards, helicopters from Chivenor and, in particular, the Appledore lifeboat crew. The *Green Ranger* joined the wrecks of over 136 vessels lost on this stretch of coast in 200 years.

The Path continues past Hole Rock, alongside Milford Common and over a most peculiar stile (which seems to have been constructed from the remains of a kitchen range), after the turn off to Elmscott Youth Hostel, before the Path runs out to a tarmac road at Sandhole Cliff. Return to the Path again after 270 metres through a large field gate on the right. However, if you are walking during harvest time, watch that you do not miss the signpost as the hay-trailer is generally parked in front of it. The Path now climbs round Nabor Point offering incredible views inland as far as the tors of Dartmoor and a wide sweeping panoramic view of all that is best in the Devon country-side, creating an incredible feeling of space and freedom.

Speke's Mi
Mouth waterfa

The Path now runs eastward and then turns away west to Embury Beacon and its Iron Age camp excavated in 1973 to uncover domestic pottery and old timbers that once formed part of dwelling huts and cattle pens. Each year more of the camp disappears into the sea, and very little remains today. The Path curves around the camp but it is possible to walk through it. It continues on to Knap Head before starting the descent into Welcombe – the last Devon valley before the Cornish border.

Welcombe Mouth, over the past few years, has become a very popular visiting place owing to its sands at low tide and grassy banks protected by twin headlands. It has gorse- and heather-clad slopes running down to a series of cascades and pools before the Strawberry Water plunges to the beach. It now has a dirt road almost to the sands and the peace and tranquility of past years has gone for ever.

Cross the stepping stones, following the Path on its last extremely steep climb to the heights above Marsland Mouth. Go over a stile, providing an opportunity for one last look back along the North Devon and Somerset coast, before plunging down past a brick built hut. The descent past the hut is very steep and should be taken with great care.

Ahead, as you descend, lies the coastline of Cornwall already changing in character from that over which we have walked. This is where Gull Rock points the way to Morwenstow with its beautiful church of St. Morwenna, and the eccentricities of its Victorian vicar (the Reverend R. S. Hawker, vicar from 1834 to 1875), who built his own hut from flotsam and jetsam on what is now Vicarage Cliff, and where he sat to write and look out over the splendours of this Cornish land- and seascape.

But all this is the subject of another guide and another walk.

Our route ends by taking the Path to the left along the valley to where the Old Smithy Inn welcomes us with refreshment and, if you are lucky, tales of Caleb Wakely, the last village blacksmith here before it became an inn. He, when not shoeing horses, would happily pull the teeth of the local populace. What better way to rest and relax, take off your boots and contemplate the joys you have experienced, before planning your next venture along the Coast Path?

Maps reference

ROADS AND PATHS

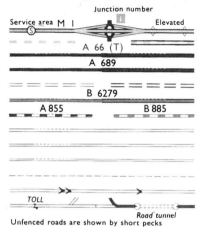

Junction number

Service area M

Elevated

Motorway

Motorway projected; under construction

A 66 (T) — Trunk road

A 689 — Main road

Under construction

} Single and dual carriageway

B 6279 — Secondary road

A 855 — B 885 — Narrow road with passing places

4·3 metres of metalling or over (not included above)

Under 4·3 metres of metalling tarred and untarred

Minor road in towns, drive or track (unmetalled)

Path

Gradients: 1 in 5 and steeper   1 in 7 to 1 in 5

TOLL

Road tunnel

Toll gate   Other gates   Entrances to road tunnels

Unfenced roads are shown by short pecks

PUBLIC RIGHTS OF WAY

.... Footpath

— — — — — — Bridleway

} Public paths

┬ ┴ ┬ ┴ ┬ ┴ ┬ ┴ Road used as a public path

Public rights of way indicated by these symbols have been derived from Definitive Maps as amended by later enactments or instruments held by Ordnance Survey and are shown subject to the limitations imposed by the scale of mapping

The representation on this map of any other road, track or path is no evidence of the existence of a right of way

RAILWAYS

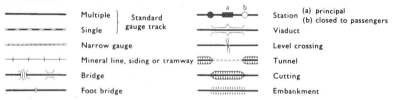

Multiple

} Standard gauge track

Single

Narrow gauge

Mineral line, siding or tramway

Bridge

Foot bridge

a   b — Station (a) principal (b) closed to passengers

Viaduct

Level crossing

Tunnel

Cutting

Embankment

WATER FEATURES

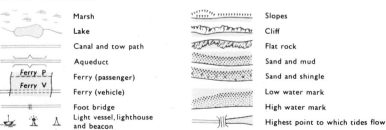

Marsh

Lake

Canal and tow path

Aqueduct

Ferry P — Ferry (passenger)

Ferry V — Ferry (vehicle)

Foot bridge

Light vessel, lighthouse and beacon

Slopes

Cliff

Flat rock

Sand and mud

Sand and shingle

Low water mark

High water mark

Highest point to which tides flow

GENERAL FEATURES

⟶ᵛ⟶ᵛ⟶	Electricity transmission line (with pylons spaced conventionally)
> – –> – –>	Pipe line (arrow indicates direction of flow)
	Quarry
	Open pit
	Wood
	Orchard
	Park or ornamental grounds
	Bracken, heath and rough grassland
	Dunes

Å	Broadcasting station (mast or tower)
�	Bus or coach station
⌿	Church ⎰ with tower
⌿	or ⎱ with spire
+	Chapel ⎰ without tower or spire
△	Triangulation pillar
⋈	Windmill (in use)
⚲	Windmill (disused)
Ⲧ	Wind pump
▲	Youth hostel

RELIEF

— 76 —

Contour values are given to the nearest metre. The vertical interval is, however, 50 feet

144

Heights are to the nearest metre above mean sea level. Heights shown close to a triangulation pillar refer to the station height at ground level and not necessarily to the summit. Details of the summit height may be obtained from the Ordnance Survey

1 metre = 3·2808 feet   15·24 metres = 50 feet

BOUNDARIES

– + — + — +	National	·—·—·—·—	County, Region or Islands Area
–○– ○– ○– ○–	London Borough	+ + + +	District
	National Park or Forest Park	················	Civil Parish or equivalent

NT   National Trust always open

ABBREVIATIONS

P	Post office	TH	Town hall, Guildhall or equivalent	
PH	Public house	PC	Public convenience (in rural areas)	
CH	Club house	.T	⎰	PO
.MP	Mile post	.A	Telephone call box ⎰	AA
.MS	Mile stone	.R	⎱	RAC

ANTIQUITIES

VILLA	Roman	+	Site of antiquity
𝕮umulus	Non-Roman	⚔ 1066	Battlefield (with date)

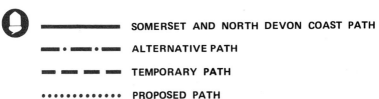

SOMERSET AND NORTH DEVON COAST PATH

ALTERNATIVE PATH

TEMPORARY PATH

PROPOSED PATH

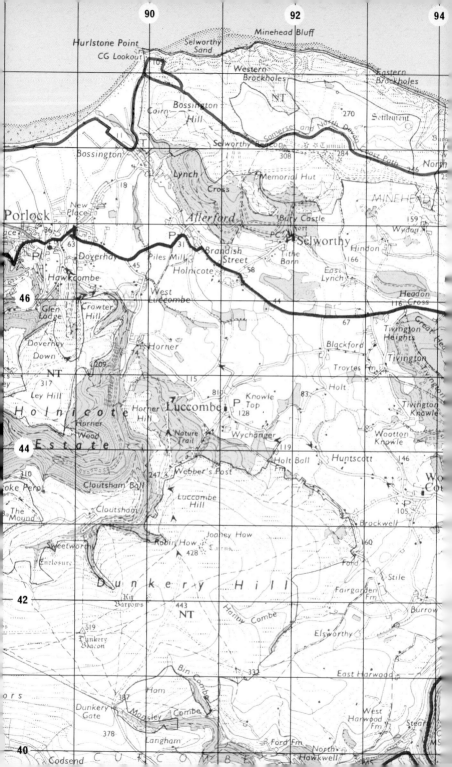

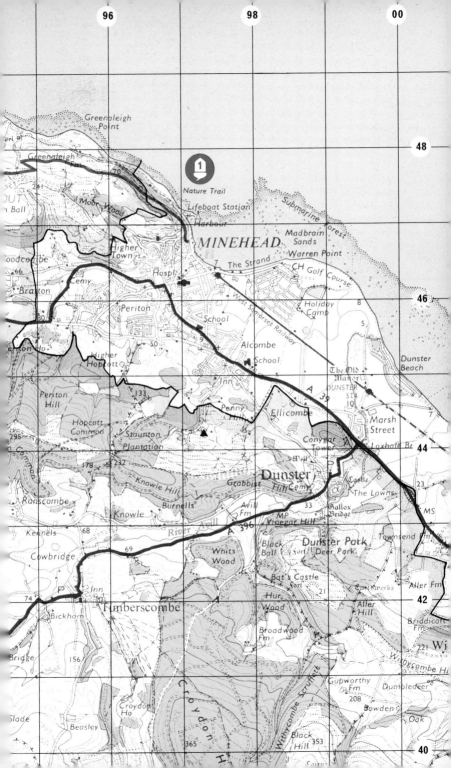

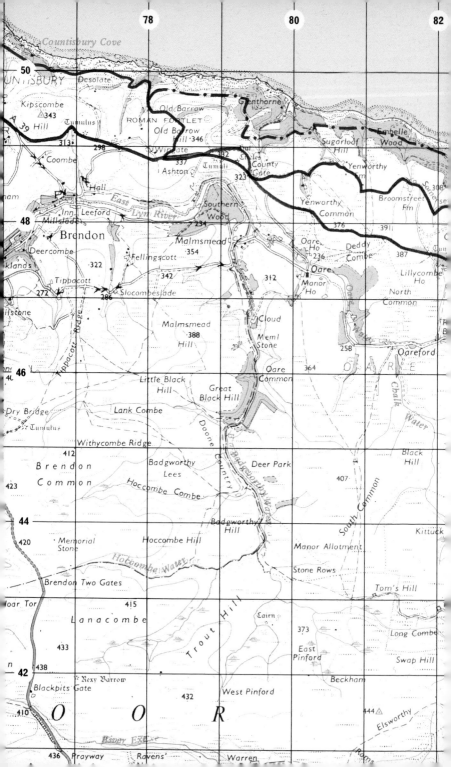

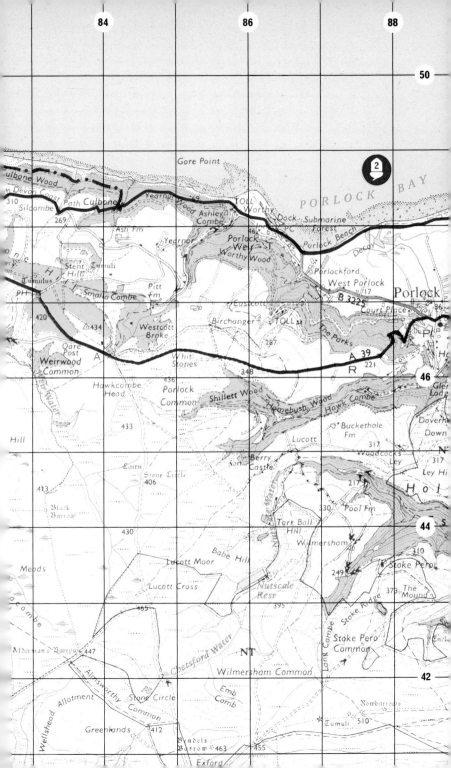

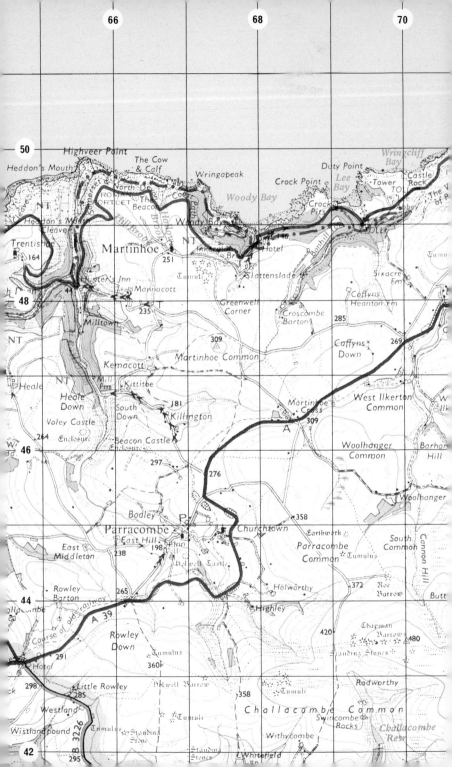

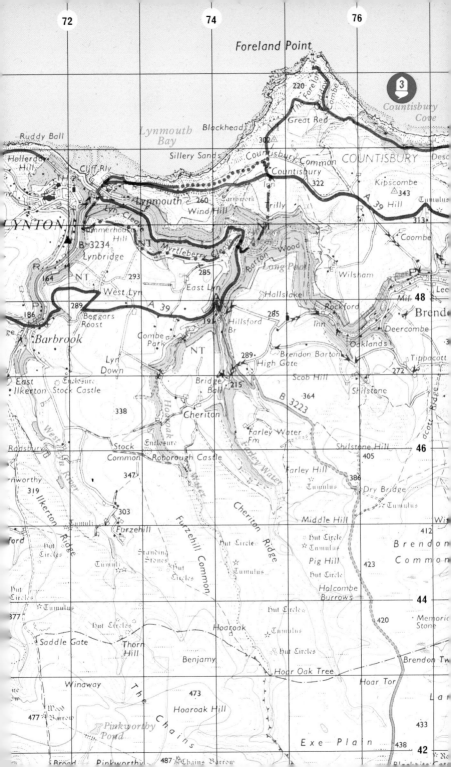

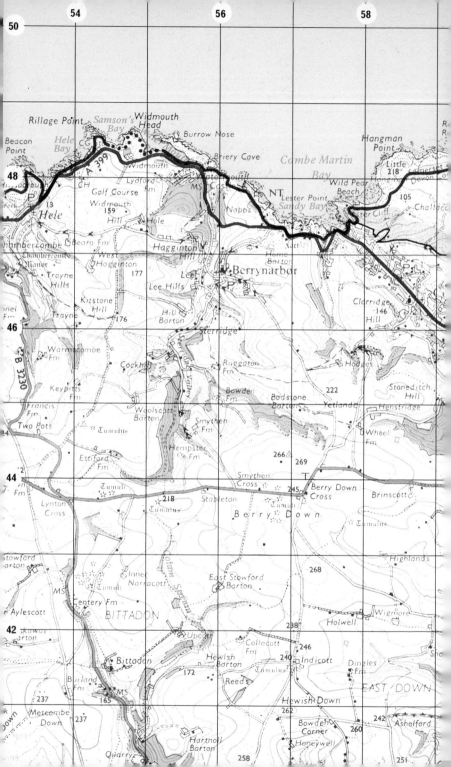

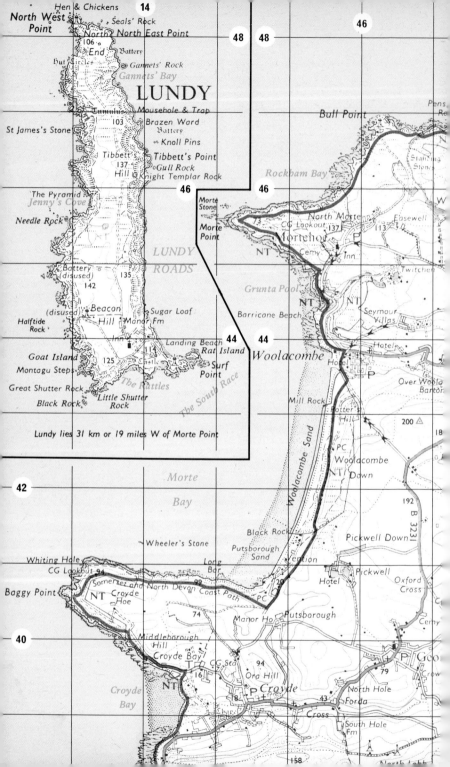

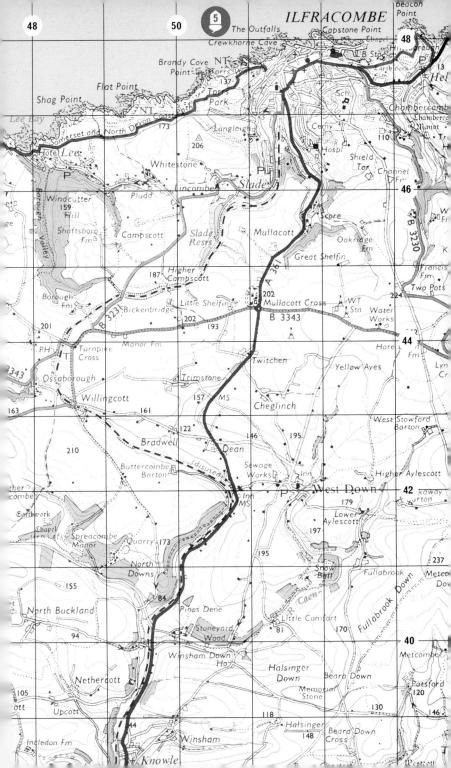

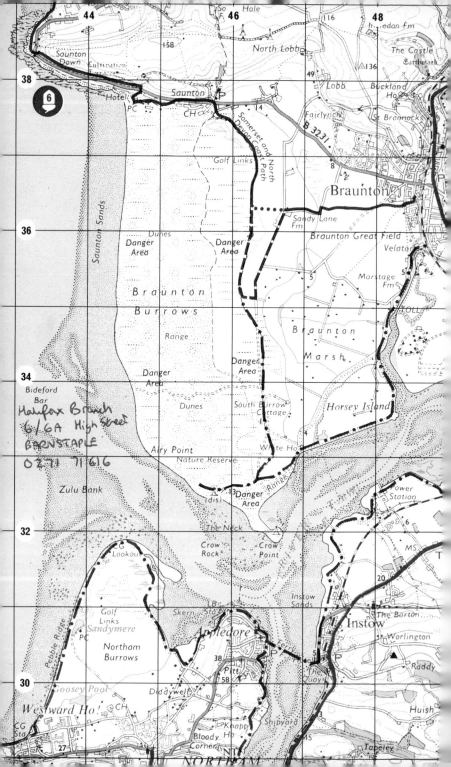

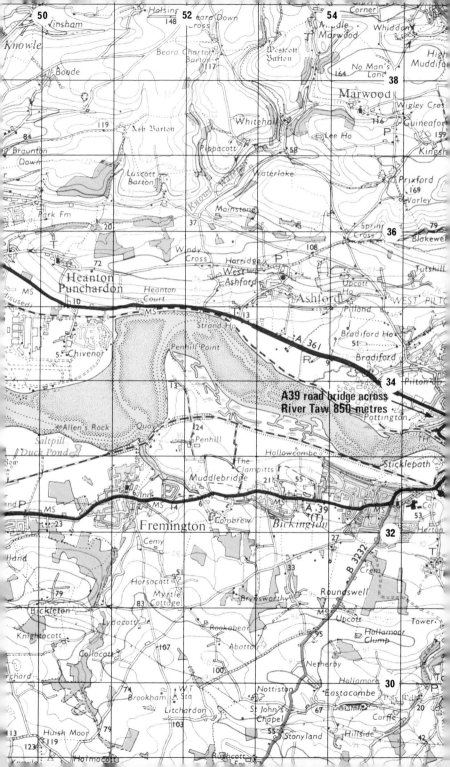

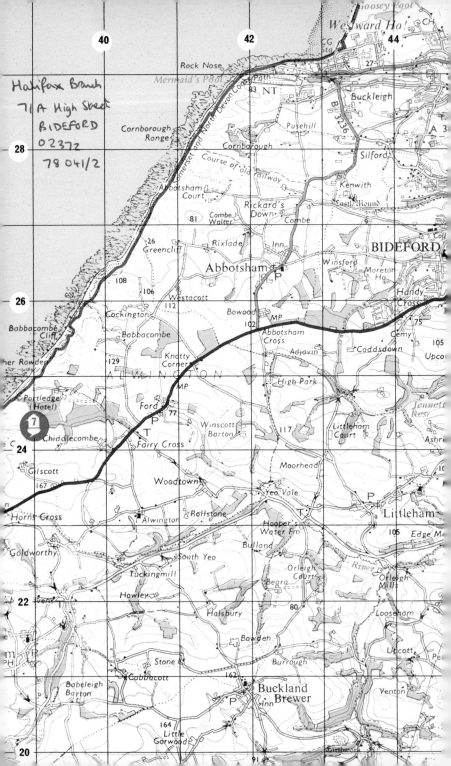

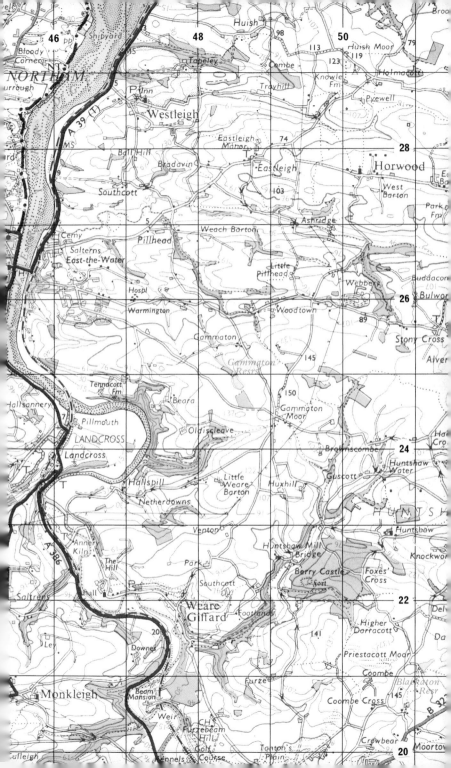

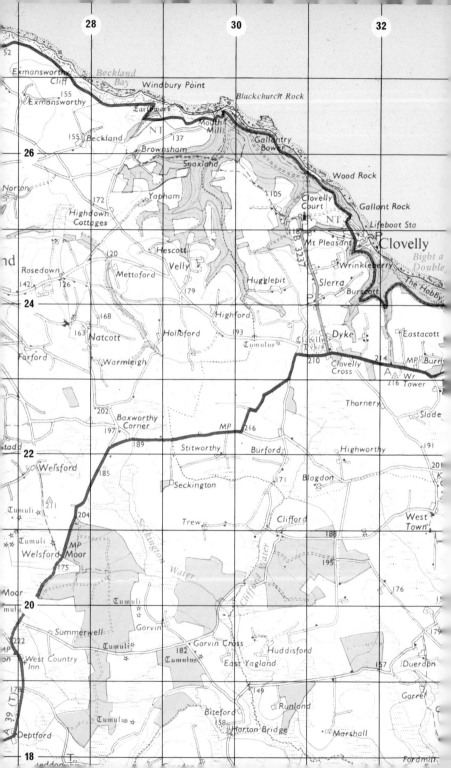

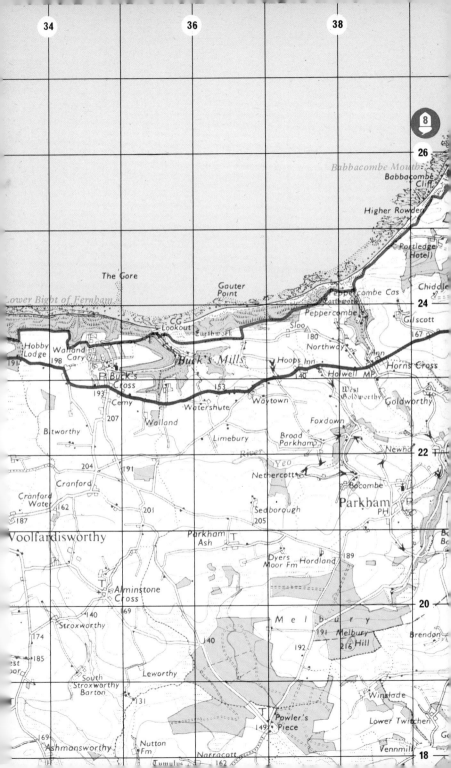

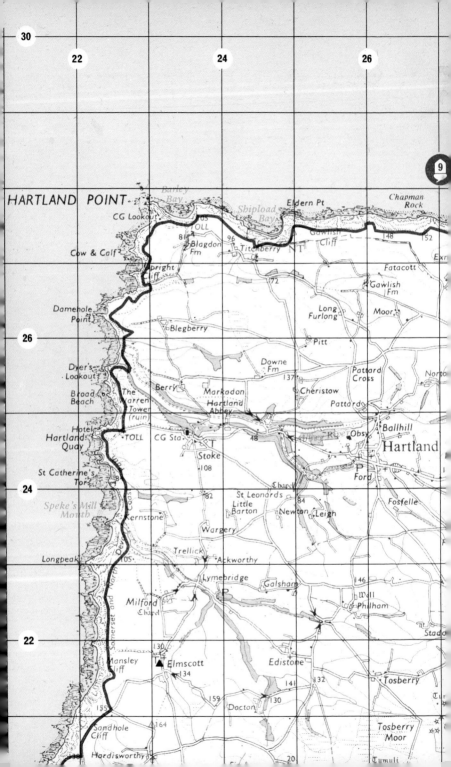

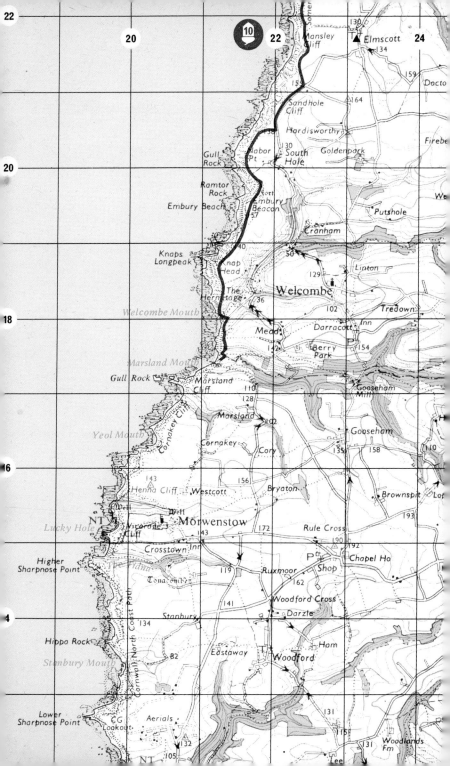

Places to visit

A brief gazeteer of towns, villages, houses and other places of interest, in order of the Coast Path route from Minehead to Marsland Mouth.

Dunster Visible from Minehead, with the tower of Conegar folly providing a landmark for the surrounding countryside. Its famous castle high above the village was rebuilt after the Norman Conquest by William de Mohun, but most of the building is of a later period. The gatehouse with four flanking towers was built during the reign of Henry V (1413–1422). The Luttrell family purchased the Manor of Dunster in 1376 and a branch of the family still live there although it is now handed over to the National Trust. The delightful village boasts a unique two-in-one church – the Monks' Church and the Peoples' Church – dating back over 500 years. The quaint octagonal building in the High Street is the Yarn Market, erected in 1609 when wool was made into cloth in this area and kersey-mere, a fine twill cloth of local wool, was marketed here.

Luccombe Lying under Dunkery Beacon and sur-rounded by wooded slopes, the name means 'shut-in-combe'. The church has fine carved and painted roof bosses. To the left of the handsome lychgate are pretty thatched cottages.

Cleeve Abbey Founded in 1188 by Cistercian monks under William de Romara, it stands on the outskirts of the village of Washford about ten kilometres from Minehead. You enter through a thirteenth-century gateway above which an inscription in Latin reads *Gate stand open nor be closed to any honest man*. Although the Abbey is partially in ruins, the refectory and chapter house are in a good state of preservation, and the roof of the refectory is beautifully carved in Spanish walnut – a wood free of worm.

Arlington Court One of the few 'stately homes' to be found on Exmoor, it stands on the east side of the A39. The house was designed by a Barnstaple man, Thomas Lee, an apprentice of Sir John Soane, in 1820. Handed over to the National Trust by the last owner, Miss Rosalie Chichester, on her death in 1949, it remains exactly as she left it. Collections of pewter, eighteenth-century furniture, and a William Blake water colour found on the top of a cupboard. There are also collections of shells, snuffboxes, crystal animals, and a fine display of model ships including Gipsy Moth IV, sailed around the world by another member of this North Devon family, Sir Francis Chichester in 1967.

Berrynarbor A pretty village of thatched cottages with well-kept gardens and a handsome twelfth- and sixteenth-century church with a red sandstone tower and seventeenth-century murals.

Barnstaple One of England's oldest boroughs and for many centuries a very important seaport and shipbuilding centre. St. Peter's Church has a thirteenth- or early fourteenth-century nave, chancel and tower, and many elaborate monuments to the wealthy mercantile families of the seventeenth century. Church Lane contains almshouses and the Maids' School, built in 1659 and endowed *for the education of 20 poor children for ever*. St. Anne's Chapel, now a small local museum, was a fourteenth-century chantry chapel and, for nearly 400 years, Barnstaple Grammar School. Here John Gay, author of *The Beggars' Opera*, was educated. Also well worth a visit are Penrose Almshouses in Litchdon Street, which have a charming courtyard and a colonnade of pillars along the road.

Tapely Park Gardens Close to Instow, about two kilometres south of the A39. Delightful gardens of rare plants with magnificent views of the surrounding land and seascapes. The gardens in the Italian style were laid out by the mother of John Christie, founder of Glyndebourne. The house contains fine furniture, porcelain and eighteenth-century plasterwork ceilings.

Bideford Built on a slope with steep, narrow lanes and alleys all running down to the tree-lined quayside along the bank of the River Torridge. Bideford was owned by

Sir Richard Grenville

105

the Grenville family from Norman times until 1744. The parish church of St. Mary dates back to Saxon times. A Norman church was built around the original small Saxon church in 1259; this was to allow services to continue uninterrupted whilst the building progressed. Today's church was built in 1862 when the Norman church was discovered to be unsafe.

Bideford's great hero was Sir Richard Grenville (1541–1591), cousin to Sir Walter Raleigh. Sir Richard took five vessels from Appledore to battle with the Armada. He died fighting 15 Spanish ships in the Azores aboard the *Revenge* and is immortalized by Tennyson in the poem of that name, which gives a romantic rather than a factual rendering of the event. Grenville also figures in Charles Kingsley's novel *Westward Ho!*

Bideford's famous bridge has 24 arches all of different widths. (Two at the west end fell into the river during 1968.) The bridge was built in 1699 to replace an earlier wooden bridge. The seventeenth and eighteenth centuries were Bideford's most prosperous period, when it carried on a flourishing trade with the American colonies.

Abbotsham A small village between Westward Ho! and Clovelly. The church of St. Helen is thirteenth-century and still has its original wagon roof, nave and chancel – it also contains some finely carved bench ends.

Hartland Despite its remoteness, Hartland supports a flourishing, almost self-sufficient community. There is an annual carnival, held after harvesting. Although only a small community, it boasts a town band, a male voice choir and some very sociable pubs, as well as a new art and music centre in The Square. This occupies the old chapel used when the locals were unable to walk to their parish church of St. Nectan at Stoke, three kilometres to the west of the town. The church was built in 1055, but was replaced around 1360 and its 39-metre high tower provides a fine view and explains the church's position which was to act as a landmark for ships using the Channel. The church contains a superb Norman font carved at the top with four heads of those saved through baptism gazing down on the upturned faces of the damned. There is also a modern memorial to Sir Allen Lane, founder of Penguin Books.

Doone Country

The Doones existed only in the imagination of Richard Dodderidge Blackmore. But a wild race of men did live in this area in the late seventeenth century, and two centuries later, Blackmore immortalized them in his novel *Lorna Doone.*

R. D. Blackmore was descended from a family with centuries old connections with Exmoor. They owned Court Barton and East Bodley in Parracombe, also Killington in Martinhoe parish.

Blackmore's *Doone Valley* is thought, by common consent, to be the entrance to Lank Combe on the west bank of Badgworthy Water.

Other *Lorna Doone* landmarks along the Coast Path may be visited at:

Porlock. *The Ship Inn* where Tom Faggus once sought refuge, escaping by whistling up his mare Winnie and galloping through his pursuers. Jan Ridd's father was murdered by the Doones at the top of Porlock Hill, and Jan bought powder and shot at the *Sign of the Spit and Gridiron*.

Oare. *Parsonage Farm*, where Blackmore wrote a great deal of the novel. Also the scene of a dreadful murder in the book. *Oare Manor*, then Lorna Doone Farm, where Farmer Snow lived. *Oare Church*, where Jan Ridd and Lorna were married although, owing to restoration in past years, it is no longer possible to line up a shot from a window to the altar, as in the novel.

Glenthorne. *Yenworthy Farm*, close to the Coast Path, on the way to County Gate. The farm still possesses an enormous gun, said to be that used by the Widow Fisher against the Doones raiding the farm, firing the hay ricks to try and entice the occupants out in order to rob the building.

Valley of Rocks. *Mother Meldrun's Cave* where, one cold winter's day, Jan Ridd came visiting her refuge in the cave beneath the weird-shaped rock-pile known as the Devil's Cheese-ring, seeking her advice in his love-affair with Lorna Doone.

Accommodation and transport

The South West Way Association publishes an annual guide to the whole of the South West Peninsula Coast Path. The information includes an accommodation list, a list of ferry operators and a timetable of ferries with advice on how to cross when they are not running. The Membership Secretary is Mrs. D. Y. Lancey, 'Kynance', Old Newton Road, Kingskerswell, Newton Abbot, Devon.

Bus services in the area are operated by Western National Omnibus Co. Ltd. Priced timetables can be obtained from National House, Queen Street, Exeter EX4 3TF (*Devon*) and from Tower Street, Taunton, Somerset (*Somerset and Dorset*).

The Ramblers' Association, 1–5 Wandsworth Road, London SW8 2LJ publish an annual *Bed and Breakfast Guide;* the English Tourist Board publish the annual *Where to Stay: West Country*, available from bookshops; and the West Country Tourist Board, Trinity Court, Southernhay East, Exeter EX1 1QS produce annual lists of accommodation.

There are five youth hostels convenient to the route. Details of membership and opening times can be obtained from the Youth Hostels Association, Trevelyan House, St. Stephen's Hill, St. Albans, Hertfordshire AL1 2DY or direct from the wardens.

Youth Hostels

Minehead Alcombe Combe: less than two kilometres up Alcombe Combe from Bridgwater–Minehead road. Turn off main road into Church Street or Brook Street past Britannia Inn by Manor Road. Hostel 400 metres on left beyond gate-posts of a private road.
Bus from Bridgwater, Taunton, Exeter, Lynmouth.

Exford The Mead, Exford: in the village, next to the river bridge on the Withypool road.
Bus Minehead–Wheddon Cross. Minehead–Porlock.
Coach London–Taunton. Minehead–Exford. Ilfracombe.

Lynton Lynbridge, Lynton: approached by Lynway opposite Ye Olde Cottage Inn between top of Lynmouth Hill and Barbrook. From Lynton take steps opposite church up Sinai Hill about 50 metres, then left along Lynway.
Railway Station Barnstaple.
Bus Lynton–Fountain Cross–Barnstaple. All year. Lynton–Fountain Cross–Ilfracombe. Summer only. Lynmouth–Minehead. Summer only.

Instow Worlington House, Instow: turn off main Barnstaple–Bideford road in Instow at signpost. Youth Hostel 800 metres.
Railway Station Barnstaple.
Coach London–Bideford–Barnstaple.
Bus Bideford–Barnstaple every 30 minutes – alight Marine Hotel.

Elmscott Elmscott, Hartland: west of Hartland village, footpath through top of St. Leonard's Valley. From Bude, Kilkhampton, first left immediately beyond West Country Inn.
Railway Station Barnstaple.
Bus Bideford–Hartland.

Squirrel and rabbits, with buzzards overhead

A short book list

Devon: A Shell Guide by John Betjeman, revised by Brian Watson. Faber & Faber.

Lorna Doone by R. D. Blackmore.

The Naturalist in Devon and Cornwall by Roger Burrows. David & Charles.

Exmoor by S. H. Burton. Hodder & Stoughton.

Exmoor ed. by John Coleman-Cooke. HMSO.

British Regional Geology – South West England by E. A. Edmonds, MSc, M. C. McKeown, BSc, M. Williams, BSc, PhD. HMSO.

South West England by Aileen Fox. David & Charles.

The Archaeology of Exmoor by L. V. Grimsell. David & Charles.

Selected Writings by William Hazlitt. Penguin.

Flowers of the Coast by Ian Hepburn. William Collins (New Naturalist).

The Making of the English Landscape by W. G. Hoskins. Pelican.

Devon by W. G. Hoskins. Collins.

Westward Ho! by Charles Kingsley. Macmillan.

Stalky & Co. by Rudyard Kipling. Macmillan.

The King's England: Devon by Arthur Mee. Hodder & Stoughton.

The Reclamation of Exmoor Forest by C. S. Orwin and R. J. Sellack. David & Charles.

Portrait of Exmoor by J. H. B. Peel. Robert Hale.

The Buildings of England: North Devon by Nikolaus Pevsner. Penguin.

The Sea Coast by J. A. Steers. Collins (New Naturalist).

Fossils by H. H. Swinnerton. Collins (New Naturalist).

Geology and Scenery in England and Wales by A. E. Trueman. Pelican.

The Walkers' Handbook by H. D. Westacott. Penguin.

Life of the Shore and Shallow Sea by Douglas P. Wilson, DSc, FRPS. Nicholas & Watson.

The Sea Shore by C. M. Yonge. Collins (New Naturalist).

Near Hartland Quay, looking towards Screda Point

The Country Code

Guard against all risk of fire

Fasten all gates

Keep dogs under proper control

Keep to the paths across farm land

Avoid damaging fences, hedges and walls

Leave no litter

Safeguard water supplies

Protect wild life, wild plants and trees

Go carefully on country roads

Respect the life of the countryside

And please do not leave bottles, tins, and litter after your picnic – it is unsightly and broken glass and jagged tins may cause injury to children and animals.

Ditchers, Bossington